The Reformation of Halloween

By Phil Wyman

Cover Photo: Peter Heeling. Creative Commons Zero license through Pexels.com.

Author Photos: Michelle Rogers Pritzl

The Reformation of Halloween

Introduction to this Crazy Book on Halloween

This small book describes a positive Christian engagement with the strange American holiday we call Halloween. The ideas here were hatched like an alien that had been incubating over thirty years, and the experiences were born in the context of being a pastor in Charismatic and Evangelical churches. Eighteen of those years were in a small city that is notoriously considered Halloween Central: Salem, Massachusetts.

My first fourteen years pastoring were spent in Carlsbad, California. We had a small church in Carlsbad, with lots of kids, and in the mid 1980's, I had to determine how our church would deal with the subject of Halloween. What would we tell the families? How would the church interact with this popular holiday? The 80's were particularly critical years for this subject, and my response was important to people in the church.

The 1980's were critical, because they were filled with fear, and Halloween was not the only target of dangerous stories and deadly urban myths. A whole score of things that we had once taken for granted were now perceived through the eyes of suspicion. It wasn't just the Christian church that rose to frenzied concerns over things happening in our world, society as a whole was haunted by demons hiding behind every rock.

The 1980's brought an end to hitchhiking. That grand old institution that once got you to the beach as a teenager, or a ride to your first job on the other side of town, that allowed hippies to hitch across country for concerts, or allowed people to travel Europe on just $5 a day was now becoming an object of horror stories. Drivers were afraid to pick up the travelers with their thumbs sticking out. HBO's horror mystery, "The Hitchiker", and urban myths about serial killers hitchhiking buried themselves into the public psyche, and this institution of American culture slowly disappeared along with a little bit of trust in our neighbors and their children.

Even while hitchhiking dissolved in front of our eyes, and moved toward near extinction, Halloween was faced with similarly fearsome stories. Parents were afraid of poisoned candy, and apples with razorblades. We were told that Witches' covens were supposedly sacrificing animals, and harvesting babies for sacrifice in the 1980's. At this same time, a satanic ritual abuse scare made it's way through the churches of America and the U.K. Mike Warnke had already kicked off the scare in US churches. In 1972, Warnke and his book, The Satan Seller, made its way through the churches of America. Later the secular world would be rocked with the same fears. Michelle

Remembers was published in 1980. It told stories of the Satanic Ritual Abuse (SRA) of Michelle Smith as told by her and her Psychologist – soon to be husband – Lawrence Pazder. In 1983, the McMartin Preschool case in Manhattan Beach, California kicked off a panic about a supposed underground of Satanists running daycare centers and abusing children throughout the US. Psychology, religion, education, and even law enforcement would be affected by these fears, and it would take 10-20 years for many of the allegations to be shown to be wildly exaggerated and sometimes completely false, but by then, transformation had already occurred in our culture. We were not the open and caring people we used to be. We were closed to our neighbors, and fearful that a child molester, or a Satanist was just around the corner or waiting in the next aisle at the grocery store.

During this season of fear mongering, Neo-Paganism (a fast growing religion with people who have titles like Witch, Pagan, Druid, Heathen and a variety of other religious monikers) would become a primary target. Neo-Pagans would be accused of cursing churches, abusing children, and sacrificing animals. These accusations, like those of the McMartin Case turned out to be unfounded, but by the time authorities realized how unfounded the accusations were, it was already too late. Hollywood, Christian churches, and the general populace had made their decision. They were convinced something malevolent and violent was beneath the surface of these alternative religions.

Halloween, with its attachment to scary costumes and tales of ghosts, monsters, witches, and a host of supernatural beings, naturally became a target for some of these same fears. As Halloween grew in popularity, it also grew in notoriety in churches, and Christians became afraid of it. It is surprising that Halloween not only survived, but flourished and grew exponentially during this same season of fear. The family friendly dynamics of Halloween and the satanic scare were counterposed against one another, but it appears that it was primarily the Church that feared Satanists and Witches during Halloween. The common public continued celebrating the holiday, and did so with a gusto that created a phenomenal growth in the holiday.

As a new pastor, I had to decide very early in my pastoral work how I, and we as a church, should respond to Halloween. September 1, 1985 was my first day pastoring the small church in Carlsbad, California, and Halloween was just around the corner.

As will be evident in this book, I try to do everything I can to get the church to extend itself outside the walls of her meeting place, and to engage with the world around us in meaningful, redemptive – and even fun ways. So, my first Halloween as a pastor was no exception. Our small church had a handful of people who wanted to share the Gospel with others, so I suggested that we go "Tract-or-Treating." On Halloween night 1985, in the heat of this season of satanic scare, myself and a dozen other people, with some of their children, went door-to-door in my neighborhood singing hymns like a group of Christmas Carolers.

I returned with a guitar full of candy – and money that people insisted on donating in spite of my protests. The neighbors loved our Tract-or-Treating, and so did our little church, and this was the beginning of my relationship with Halloween in a positive Christian engagement. Over the next fourteen years in Carlsbad, our Halloween grew into a Great Pumpkin Festival in the Girl's Club where we met on Sunday mornings. Now it included an invitation to a much larger neighborhood.

But then, everything suddenly changed: I moved to Salem, Massachusetts in 1999 to start a new church. Now I lived in a city with over a dozen Witchcraft shops. Thousands of people who self-identified as Witches or Neo-Pagans lived in the city. What's more, Salem boasted thirty-one days of Halloween. The entire month of October was one big Halloween called Haunted Happenings.

It might not be a stretch to say, that I just might have more experience than any other pastor in history in getting Christians involved with this strange American holiday we call Halloween. I have been working with Christians from around the world on the streets of Salem during the month-long Halloween event for almost 20 years. This book comes from 19 years, of month-long Halloweens. That's close to 600 Halloween days, and only counts the actual days of the month of October – not any of the year round preparation that goes into it. Thousands of people have come to Salem, and been trained to get involved with our Halloween in meaningful, redemptive, and fun ways.

Needless to say, this simple little book will have its detractors, but that's familiar territory for me. Martin Luther and I share the same birthday – you know – the guy who was chased around Europe by the Pope and his men for suggesting reforms to the Catholic Church. He and I also have something else in common: We both have done a lot of work on Halloween Day. Martin Luther nailed his 95 theses to the Wittenburg Door on Reformation Day, which happens to be Halloween. As for me, well, I suppose this is my thesis on why we need a reformation over how the church engages with Halloween.

Phil Wyman
July 31, 2018

Table of Contents

A Short – No, a VERY Short History of Halloween

Okay, I know that my use of the word "very" above is a very bad thing for a writer to do, just like I did again in this sentence. But, there is a reason I used "very" in this way.

We do not have a word like "very" in our snobby American-English literary tradition, which is a very strange thing to say (see I did it again!), because it is like saying that there is no word for "very" in English. It's like a ghost that appears regularly, but isn't supposed to exist.

Your work will get thrown into the circular file by an editor or literary agent for using the word "very" in a manuscript. That is the kind of distain writers have for the word "very." Instead we have to use comparatives and superlatives. We say "faster" or "fastest", and "taller" or "tallest." When there are more complex patterns where single word comparatives and the superlatives don't quite fit, we have to come up with other creative ways to make something bigger than life. It cannot be a "very long way." It has to be an "unimaginably tiring distance." Someone cannot be "very enthusiastic"; they must be "ebullient". Whatever that means.

I speak Welsh. The Welsh language is the most vibrant and living of the Celtic languages today, and although Welsh has comparatives and superlatives, it also has an equivalent for the popular street version of the word – hated by writers – "very." It is the word "iawn", which rhymes with "town". But, iawn is an even larger word, it can also mean correct or right, and nicely stands alone as a response or question.

"Iawn" is so popular in Welsh that it has transferred over, and influenced how the Welsh speak English. The Welsh love to say things are "very" or "really". If you imagine the words with a heavy emphasis on the first syllable and a rolled r – VEHry, or "Rrrrreeea-ly" and hear them saying it twice, then you have a sense of how much the Welsh like to make things bigger than life.

"O no, we don't go there too often, it's a very, very long way."

"But it's only the next town over."

"Ah, but you have to go around the mountain. The sheep are always in the road if you go that way."

"O, that's a really nice paned (cup of tea – pronounced like your Pa's name is Ned)."

"And the biscuits are really, really nice too."

Having said all that about my use of the word "very", now I will get to the point. I used the word, because in that beautiful Celtic tongue, Welsh, there is a word for our common – despised by academics – use of the word "very." And, the history of American Halloween goes back to ancient Celtic times, or at least that is the assumption made by people who like to talk about the ancient history of Halloween, and when they talk about it they make it very, very, really, really evil sounding.

Now, to quote a not so very academic, but surprisingly smart Wikipedia post on Halloween, let's begin the discussion:

> *It is widely believed that many Halloween traditions originated from ancient Celtic harvest festivals, particularly the Gaelic festival Samhain & Brythonic festival Calan Gaeaf: that such festivals may have had pagan roots; and that Samhain itself was Christianized as Halloween by the early Church. Some believe, however, that Halloween began solely as a Christian holiday, separate from ancient festivals like Samhain.*[1]

So, here's the point of using the Wiki quote: We don't really know the history of ancient Halloween, or of its modern variation.

People wax eloquent about what the ancient Druids did in Wales and Ireland, but we don't know for sure. Heck, we are not even sure what happened at Stonehenge. Some of the most recent thoughts are

---

[1] https://en.wikipedia.org/wiki/Halloween (Aug 8, 2018)

that people came from Wales across the Salisbury plains to build this site, but archeologists are not sure why. Why there? Why then?

If we can't figure out the basic information about a massive stone formation that we can still visit today, what makes us think that we can have accurate information on a holiday celebration happening in mid-autumn in Ireland and Wales during the years when we have little to no written history? Even the idea that ancient Druids were sacrificing humans comes from a couple questionable sources written by the Romans, who were justifying their slaughter of the Britons. You know, the same way in which the victor always writes the history. As historian Ronald Hutton says about the ancient practices of Samhain and Noson Galan Gaeaf, "we have virtually no idea".[2]

Here's the real take away: If we don't know what truly happened in ancient Ireland and Wales with the Druids and their Samhain, and Noson Galan Gaeaf gatherings, how are we to trust those who tell us that ancient pagans did terrible things on Halloween, and that our participation in Halloween is connected to this ancient Pagan practice?

On the flip side of this story, it is also believed that ancient Welsh Druids were among the first Saints during what has been called the Age of the Saints in the Celtic lands. If this is true, then we are demonizing the same people who may have been the impetus for one of the greatest missionary movements in the history of the world.

---

[2]https://www.theguardian.com/commentisfree/2014/oct/28/halloween-more-than-trick-or-treat-origins (Sept. 8, 2018)

It seems wise to me, assuming that we know so little about the ancient history of Halloween that we cannot presumptuously say that Halloween in America is based upon ancient Pagan celebrations with sacrifices to false gods and goddesses. To accuse parents, who are taking their kids trick-or-treating for Halloween, of being practitioners of some ancient Pagan ritual is outright audacious, and very, very annoying. Iawn?

As far as the more recent history of Halloween in North America, the oldest record of children dressing up in costume and going door to door is 1911 in Ontario, Canada. The practice is a relatively recent historical development in North America. Halloween grew into the phenomenon it has become in American culture from the 1920's to the 1950's, with a short break for sugar rationing during World War II. Its source is almost certainly connected to All Hallows Eve, which is the evening before All Souls Day. This makes the North American Halloween more closely related to Christianity than to any other religion.

So, in truth, Halloween as we practice it is young holiday. It does not have an ancient, dark and evil history. The best we can do in tracking its origins and development is to look back over its short history.

Over the course of the 20th century, Halloween slowly developed into a family-friendly event with children roving from neighbor to neighbor shouting, "trick-or-treat" and receiving candy from those who answered the doors. There was some fear of violence among young hoodlums in the beginning of the 20th century, but the holiday was promoted as a family event to counteract the hooliganism. It was not until the 60's that the scary-but-false stories of razor blades in candied apples occurred, and a short time later the association of Halloween with the newly developing Neo-Pagan Witchcraft movement, which had its beginning in the late 1940's or early 1950's, and the brand new First Church of Satan started by Anton Levay in 1966, joined the Halloween urban myths. Here is the funny thing about equating the development of Halloween in America with Neo-Pagan Witches: Halloween came first, Neo-Paganism developed much later.

Yes, Witches do celebrate Halloween. Well, they celebrate something on that same day, but what they celebrate is not what we know as the American Halloween. The next chapter will focus on the modern Pagan connections to this holiday.

As for now, it would be reasonable to say, that if Christians should be doing anything about Halloween, we should be restoring the sense of family fun, and community openness that made Halloween the big holiday that it has become, and perhaps some of us should be rediscovering the Christian origins of the holiday.

What the Witches do on Halloween

"What do children taste like?"

"I don't know, but I would imagine they taste like chicken."

– a Witch from the WLPA talking to a Salem visitor

The Witchcraft League for Public Awareness (WLPA) was far more active a couple decades ago. It was formed by Salem Witch Lori Cabot and fellow Witches for the purpose of dispelling myths about the practices and beliefs of modern day Witches. It was common during Halloween, to find the WLPA at a table in downtown Salem answering questions, and helping little kids make wands for their Halloween costumes.

Today, some of the witchcraft shops in Salem are still putting out tables and answering public questions about Witchcraft. One of the local Witches, an acquaintance of mine, says that even though the public perception of Salem's Witches has improved, people still ask silly questions like, "What do children taste like?" or, "Do you practice human sacrifice?" One day, she pondered out loud, "How do you even answer questions like that without being rude?"

So, if Witches are not eating children or sacrificing virgins and kitty cats on Halloween, what are they doing? And how does it affect the holiday?

October 31st is a date that has a few different celebrations around the world attached to it.

In Mexico, it is the Day of the Dead. Dia de Muertos supposedly has pre-Spanish colonization roots reaching back into Aztec culture and the honoring of departed relatives. As the Catholic Church filled every corner of Mexico, it took Dia de Muertos (or as we call it in America "Dia de los Muertos") and merged it with the already long celebrated All Saints' Day. The day was more about remembering dearly departed family members than about dark demonic purposes.

Samhain (sɑːwɪn) is a Gaelic festival with roots in ancient Ireland, Scotland and the Isle of Man. It is believed to have ancient Pagan origins, but there is no certainty about the ceremonies and rituals surrounding the day. Similarly there was a Noson Galan Gaeaf in Wales, and its ancient ceremonial aspects are equally shrouded in mystery. It is only as recently as the late 19th century that Sir James Frazer suggested that this was the Celtic New Year, and that idea has gained traction and been repeated by other scholars since.

In Irish mythology, Samhain was a day when doors to the otherworld were opened and spirits gained access to the earth. Great gatherings with drinking and celebrations and contests are mentioned in old tales. Some tales suggest offerings and sacrifices were made during this time. Historian Ronald Hutton suggests that Pagan rites are likely to have been associated with Samhain, but he believes that the tales do not really mention them.

Despite the mysterious nature of Samhain and Halloween, Neo-Pagans have adopted the holiday as their own, and it has become the highest holyday of the Celtic cycle of four festivals: Samhain (Nov. 1), Imbolc (Feb. 1), Beltane (May 1), and Lughnasah (Aug. 1).

Since the late 20th century, Neo-Pagans of all varieties have celebrated Samhain in many ways. Circles (also known as covens) gather, open public celebrations occur, and Witches' Balls are celebrated. Reconstructionists try to emulate what they believe might have happened among the ancient Celts. Wiccans celebrate it as the most important day of the four greater sabbats of the year, and see it as a day for honoring the dead. These developments are more recent than the actual celebration of Halloween itself, and the practice of trick-or-treating has no connection to any of these Neo-Pagan practices. Even the connection of Christianity to All Saints', or All Souls' Day precedes modern Witches adoption of the day as a remembrance of the departed.

It would appear that Neo-Pagans today have taken more from Christianity's celebration of the day than from anything we actually know of ancient paganism. How strange it is that Christians have been chased off from celebrating their own holiday?

The Culture of Halloween

Holidays and Festivals develop cultures of their own. Just like nations, ethnic groups, and subcultures have their own way of doing things; holidays and festivals have their rituals. They have dos and don'ts. They have preferences and unspoken rules of behavior. Christmas has its tree, its gift giving, the motif of snowy winters and Santa's elves, and the baby Jesus and manger scenes thrown in as a reminder of what we should be celebrating at Christmas. Saint Patrick's Day has its green clothing and drinking, which is probably not high on Patrick's list of things to do on the day we remember him. Similarly, Halloween has its own culture, but being a newer holiday than the others, it is still developing that culture.

Trick-or-Treating is the most common activity on Halloween. A deeper consideration of this yearly ritual reveals more than roaming neighborhoods and demanding candy.

- **Gifting** – Trick-or-Treating encourages neighbors to give to stranger's children without consideration of getting anything in return. It does not demand family connections. Halloween brings out the best in generosity. Through the simple action of placing local children at your door, Halloween gives you the opportunity to exercise your giving muscles. Giving becomes a fun event rather than a mandatory action. If the hilarious giving of Halloween were to expand itself beyond that one day of the year, it might be a benefit to our world.
- **Surprise** – the act of knocking on a door and shouting, "trick-or-treat" allows kids to practice surprising others. From a very young age, we discover that people are pleased to be surprised in innocent ways. Like a child that hides their eyes and thinks that they have become invisible to their parents, the costume and mask hide the child and give them the opportunity to extend the silly innocence of surprise beyond their toddler years. This element of surprise is something found in the Gospel itself. God surprises us with His love. He surprises us with moments of His presence. Like a knock on the door he asks to come in and sup with us. (Revelation 3:20) Halloween takes Russian philosopher Mikhail Bakhtin's theory of carnivalesque, which sees carnival surprise

as a means of turning the world upside down, and makes it a practice for everyone who participates in the day.

- **Community acceptance** – the culture of the holiday encourages people to meet their neighbors. It expands our small world to others we seldom have contact with. When we understand this as a part of the culture of Halloween, we also understand that our engagement with the holiday is an open door for redemptive relationships with others.

Costuming and the corresponding roleplaying that comes with it are fundamental to the Halloween experience.

- **By wearing masks, we drop our masks** – A strange thing happens when people wear masks and take on the character of a costume. We live in a world of people wearing existential masks to hide their fears, their guilt, and their insecurities when they go to work. Often we are even wearing masks at home with our families. When a person wears a costume during the Halloween season, he/she often expresses things about their inner identity they would normally suppress. Halloween allows many people to be more themselves than they might in everyday life. The freedom offered by wearing a mask brings honesty to the forefront in ways we may not see in our day-to-day relationships. When we understand how this occurs on Halloween we also find new opportunities to encourage personal transformation.

- **Storytelling** – costuming encourages roleplaying, and the stories of our roleplaying represent tales of heroism and supernatural intervention. Isn't this the kind of thing we wish was part of the dialogue of everyday life. Don't our hearts yearn for retelling the greatest story ever told?

Halloween is a celebration. Like so many holidays and even the holydays of Judaism and Christianity, All Hallow's Eve includes celebration as a means of honoring life and death. When you see this as part of the culture of Halloween, it allows you to see something God has placed in the hearts of all men and women: the desire to honor and celebrate life, and to celebrate it even in the face of death.

The Pastor of Halloween

The introduction already prepared you with a basic history of my pastoral experience and how it relates to Halloween. It took less than a month for me to figure out how I was going to engage with this holiday, which was perceived as the antithesis of Christian values, and I decided to face it head on.

It was Carlsbad, CA in 1985. It was during the heat of the frenzied evangelical fear of all things perceived as occult or Pagan. Halloween was one of those most feared moments, and the urban myths were many, exaggerated, and filled with visions of sacrifices, curses, and other occult dangers.

My idea of facing something "head on" is different than the traditional evangelical "head on" approach. Typically, "head on" involves bullhorns, sign waving, and sermons filled with aggressive denunciations. I decided to go "head on" by participating in the day, and by meeting others who were participating in it. My idea of "head on" is what I have called "grace in your face." It's a face-to-face engagement with lots of grace and acceptance.

Not quite two months into being a pastor of a small church, we took a group of evangelicals "Tract-or-Treating." It sounds like a pretty cheesy idea in the year 2018, but in 1985 evangelicals were being warned about participating in this diabolical holiday. They were holding prayer meetings and praying against the forces of evil they believed were doing terrible things on this high holiday of Witchcraft Covens and Satanists.

But by going out "Tract-or-Treating" we were accomplishing three things:

- We appealed to the evangelical need of the young men in our church that wanted to get out and proclaim the Gospel, and they were able to do it a non-confrontational manner.
- We brought families together with their children; families who were wondering if it was okay to let their kids participate in a community event with all their friends.
- We brought our faith outside the church walls and onto the streets, and of all things we did it on a day least expected.

Our group traveled through my new neighborhood, and knocked on doors. We sang hymns like Christmas Carolers, and received extremely warm receptions from all the neighbors. The kids received candy, and like all kids on

Halloween got terribly excited, the evangelistically-minded young men were able to sing about Jesus in public and watch their new pastor invite people to church, and we watched the neighbors fall in love with our quirky celebration of Halloween.

My poor guitar suffered the indignity of becoming a holding place for candy and money. People insisted on giving something. Because I did not have a bag, most of them used the hole in my guitar. The people greeting us in their homes stuck the candy between the strings, and my guitar increased in weight through the hour and a half of "Tract-or-Treating." Some of the people were so impressed that they wanted to give a donation to the church. When I said that it wasn't necessary, they stuffed the money between the strings as well. I returned home with just under forty dollars and about four pounds of candy.

So here were our discoveries in our first missional engagement with Halloween:

- Our neighbors loved it. They couldn't give us enough praise, and added donations to the church, as well as candy to my poor overstuffed guitar. We stood in stark contrast to the standard expectation of evangelical churches hiding away from the imagined evils of Halloween. It provided a bit of relief against the protectionary measures of the rising fundamentalism of our day.
- We discovered that we could do the Gospel and have fun at the same time. The Gospel and Fun are not mutually

independent of one another. Despite the standard angry looking approach sometimes presented by street preachers with protest placards and bullhorns, we discovered that we could share our faith in song, invite people to church and do it in silly costumes with the children in tow.

- We also discovered that it is indeed true that every day belongs to the Lord. *"This day belongs to the Lord! Let's celebrate and be glad today."* (Psalm 188:24 CEV) The Gospel is adaptable. It is not suppressed by people's celebrations. It does not care about costumes, whether we wear them or do not wear them. It is not hidden by themes of superheroes and princesses, or even horror and death. In fact, it is discovered in those same themes, and comes to life in special ways, but we'll look at the themes of Halloween in another chapter.

The first Halloween was a hit. We repeated "Tract-or-Treating", and we added another dimension to the Halloween experience the following year. We turned our two-car garage into a neighborhood fun zone for the youngest children. Halloween often feels like a holiday for kids from five to twelve years old. Those who are younger toddle around the neighborhood or have to be carried. If they can run, that is exactly what they do, and parents have a difficult time keeping them from running around like crazy with the other children in the neighborhood. For the next couple years, our little garage fun zone became a place that weary parents could stop and relax in a controlled environment. Sunday School workers from the church, who are naturally great with children and love working with them, enjoyed the opportunity of taking their experience outside the church walls.

Most of the games were simply fun and games experiences, like a plastic pool filled with plastic balls and prizes hidden in the pool. For the older kids we had classic experiences like bobbing for apples, or the more sanitary version of the apple on a string, which the child had try to take a bite out of without using his/her hands. It didn't take long for parents to join in and try their teeth at capturing an apple, and the fathers became rather competitive.

The Sunday School teachers added Bible themed games that were simply variations on lessons from Sunday School, and despite the rising trend in our culture against religious themes, parents and children loved the experience.

Over the next years, our house was not the only one providing a garage fun house in its neighborhood. Soon, other people in the church were creating Halloween events in their neighborhoods as well. One family turned their house into a haunted house for the neighborhood teen-agers. The garage fun house did not fit the age groups of their own kids and their friends, so a haunted house drew a crowd, and some of the people coming to their home haunted house started visiting our church. Here, friendly community engagement and missional outreach met in a free-flowing non-aggressive manner. Something many people once might have thought was a compromise of the faith turned into mission through friendships.

A few years into this experimental relationship with Halloween, I went to the Supermarket a week before Halloween, and the pumpkins were on sale. They were on sale for a ridiculously low-price of something like nine cents a pound. Two large cardboard boxes, big enough to put a large dining room table into, were filled with pumpkins. I dug through the boxes, and on the bottom of one box, I found the largest pumpkin I had ever seen for sale in a grocery store. I triumphantly carried it to the check out line, with other customers jealously eyeing my pumpkin, and placed in on the conveyor belt. The lady at the register had a rather confused and amazed look on her face. It did not fit on the scales, and even if it had, it weighed more than the scale could measure. She decided that the best should could do was take the highest weight on the scale, which was just under 30 lbs., and charge me the amount for that weight.

That day, I walked out of the grocery store with a beautiful 45lb. to 50lb. pumpkin for $2.85. I wasn't sure what I was going to do with it, but I knew something would come to me.

That Halloween I sat on my driveway with my big pumpkin on a rotating table. My Irish Wolfhound, Abby, sat next to me, and greeted kids and families as they came. I carved the entire story of the Gospel in pictures into my great pumpkin, and I told the story of God's love as it turned. Then I passed out candy. We had recently bought a house in the nearby city of Oceanside, and our new neighbors thanked me for my pumpkin storyboard. As one mother described it, "Thank you for providing a nice alternative to the standard scary Halloween stuff."

The following year, my Gospel pumpkin turned into a Great Pumpkin Festival. Our small church rented a Girl's Club for Sunday services, but we rented the Girl's Club for Halloween that year. We received permission from the school district to distribute flyers for our Great Pumpkin Festival, and they gave a few thousand flyers out to the teachers in the elementary schools, who in turn gave them to the students.

Over the next few years, hundreds of kids in the community would come to the Girl's Club and experience the Great Pumpkin Festival. We had a room filled with carved pumpkins telling the Gospel story, and a dozen or so fun activities with prizes for kids of all ages. Halloween had gone from a neighborhood experience to a citywide experience in a few short years.

The Halloween experience was a neighborhood event for most people growing up. It was candy, and door knocking, and costumes, and people seeing if they could dress better or decorate better than their friends. It is still a neighborhood experience across America, but the holiday has expanded so greatly that it is now a massive holiday with professional Haunted Houses in every region of the US, costume parties in bars and taverns, and month-long events and experiences organized in the larger cities. Getting outside the church walls and into the neighborhoods in the 80's and 90's was an amazing lesson in simple creative mission activities. Taking it to a larger community level with our Great Pumpkin Festival was a new level of engagement with this holiday. But, I hadn't seen anything yet…

…in a few years, Salem, Massachusetts would teach me more about Halloween, and the people who celebrate it than I could ever have imagined.

Visiting Witch City

I visited Salem on and off for a little over a decade. My first visit was in 1986, and as soon as I placed by feet on the ground I wanted to move to the quirky and wonderful little tourist city. Salem is only a half hour north of Boston by train. It is the last of the northern edge of the urban sprawl that comprises the greater Boston area. Salem feels like the heartbeat of the North Shore, well, at least to those of us who live in it, and during the time I have lived there has become a foodie destination, as well as a location for tourists interested in history, architecture, and – of course – Halloween and Witches.

My periodic visits to Salem were made to familiarize myself with the city, and prepare to eventually move there. I discovered that Salem had over a dozen Witchcraft shops. These weren't just kitschy stores designed to capture tourists interested in Halloween scares, or the history of the Witch Trials. These were legitimate Witch shops owned by Witches practicing some form of Neo-Pagan Witchcraft. Yes, there were t-shirt stores and tourist trinket shops; there were haunted houses, and museums relating to

Salem's witch history, but there were also Witchcraft shops owned by practitioners of the craft, and there were more than enough Tarot readers, astrologers, and other prognosticators to supply Hogwarts.

From 1995 to 1998, I visited Salem during the month of October to see what it was like during thé month-long Halloween. The presence of occult practitioners increased in October to match the influx of visitors. Every shop had multiple card readers and psychics to take advantage of well over 500,000 tourists flooding into the city of 42,000. There were psychic fairs, and Witches' Balls, and a host of activities including a parade with local grade schools and High School marching bands at the beginning of the month, and a Children's Day on the City Common in the middle of the month.

This was the wildest expression of Halloween I had ever seen, and yet, in many ways it was the most family-friendly Halloween I had ever seen.

Strangely, October in Salem fit all the possible stereotypes of an American Halloween. With t-shirts on every corner, and witchy trinkets, it was a kitschy tourist experience. The haunted houses, museums and the plethora of tours provided both entertainment and historical context for those looking for a touch of excitement or education. There were costume contests on the weekends – for your children and your pets. The initial parade run by the Chamber of Commerce on the first Thursday of October kicked off the month of Halloween. A Children's Day on the Common aimed at serving the local school children. These events made it a family-friendly event in a family-friendly little city. For those who were into raucous partying, the bars and taverns put on evening parties throughout the month. Scores of young adults from all over the Boston area poured into Salem to pour libations down their throats on the weekends.

But, with all these things happening, the Salem activities also encouraged the urban myths and fears about Witches and Satanists. There was the Witches' Ball, and psychic fairs along with the Witchcraft shops selling their wares of crystal balls, small packets of herbs for spells, books teaching how to practice occult magic, and ritual clothing. The non-pagan passerby was often stunned by the open and free expression of Witchcraft in the city.

The month-long Halloween in Salem was the purest expression of everything Halloween had to offer, and it was provided with steroid inflamed muscle.

Before moving to Salem, I spent four years studying Neo-Paganism from an anthropological perspective: their beliefs, social patterns, and lifestyles. I visited them in their bookshops, met with them for lunch, emailed back and forth with questions about their practices and beliefs, and went to a few of their festivals. If I was going to pastor a church in a city with a large population of Witches, I figured I had to know who they were, and what made them tick. Halloween in Salem is by no means a Pagan specific festival. There are witchcraft festivities that happen throughout the month, and there are Pagan gatherings and Pagan educational events across the city, but these only make up a part of the Halloween experience that is Salem. Many people will come to Salem and never experience these things. Many people who live in the city never experience these things. Yes, even Salem has Muggles like you and I.

Despite Halloween being larger than the Neo-Pagan experience, and the fact that the greater part of the city was not involved with witchcraft, this symbol of the Witch was a significant part of the history and the popularity of Salem. The Witch was the High School mascot. It was the symbol found on police cars and businesses throughout the city. It was, in fact, the second name for the city: Witch City.

Halloween is considered to be a most special day by most of the Witches in Salem. It is connected with the Celtic New Year, and Irish Samhain (pronounced like cow-when). It is connected to the Welsh Noson Galan Gaeaf. Many believe that this is the day when the "veil between the worlds is thinnest." The unseen world comes closest to us at this time.

After a few years of study, and getting to know modern Witches, I discovered an amazing thing: Witches are Real People Too.[3]

That point may seem incredibly simple and obvious, but in an Evangelical/Pentecostal world it was revolutionary. Witches had been lumped in with Satanists, which was an incorrect observation, and together the two groups were treated as enemies to the church. In most cases, they were regular people

---

[3] Wyman, Phil. Witches are Real People Too. Self Published. 2015.

with an alternative religion. Many of them had bad experiences with Christianity, and were seeking for a religion without the baggage, or the judgment they discovered in churches.

But, it was not the Witches who had begun the Halloween holiday in America. Halloween had begun to take on the dimensions of "Trick-or-Treating", scary monsters, and ghosts before the beginning of this modern Neo-Pagan revival, which had its birth in the late 1940's or early 1950's.

I decided even before arriving in Salem, that being afraid of Witches and of Halloween was the wrong thing to do in a city with a significant population of Witches, and a Halloween that drove its yearly economy.

A couple years before moving to Salem, I would visit the city in October to teach people who wanted to evangelize in Salem on Halloween how to treat Neo-Pagans with respect.

But along with this time of teaching, my friends from California and I decided to hit the streets ourselves. The following story has been adapted into fantasy form to highlight one of our Halloween experiences before moving into town.

Jonathan Edwards and the Carnival Barker

Time and space curve toward both the bizarre and the mundane, and when calendar and chance bring them together, Heaven and Hell collide. The ancient and the divine, the modern and the evil, the noisy and the dark, the silent and the bright: these are things, which meet in a terrible and wonderful anarchy. Nothing fits together properly when the bizarre and the mundane suddenly bump into one another. They are mortal enemies accidentally caught alone together in a dark alley face to face.

And this is the place the Carnival Barker and Jonathan Edwards found themselves. They were the noisy and the dark. They were the bizarre and the mundane. They met where the ancient, the divine, the modern, and the evil clashed in time and space. They did not belong together, but their surprising introduction and their even more surprising friendship would turn the world upside down.

That same night 30 missionaries marched through the streets of a strange little village in an overly crowded dark carnival, and just like Jonathan Edwards and the Carnival Barker, they found themselves suddenly in another world. Somehow, they were translated from a safer, more predictable place into a nightmare, but missionaries are a resilient bunch, and are typically unflappable in the face of danger. One should always have a missionary on one's zombie survival team.

For safety's sake, the missionaries stayed close together passing through the crowds of the dark carnival. Feeling millennia out of their own time, matters were complicated by the crowds of alien creatures. The sturdy missionaries assumed they had been transported into the very jaws of Hell itself. Witches in bawdy Victorian bustiers shook their ample eye-popping breasts in the faces of the young missionary men. Monsters cursed at the old praying women. Demons hissed in their faces. Contorted and bloody figures spit at them. A dragon laughed at them from the high steps of a darkened church. Yet, the missionaries reached out with their Gospel literature and gently spoke the words, "Jesus loves you," but in this village their kindness was met with a curse. Papers were torn to bits and thrown back in their faces with venom and spit.

A short distance behind the marching missionaries, the two strange friends followed. The 18th century revivalist Jonathan Edwards in his pastoral robes walked with the Carnival Barker, and the two talked among themselves about the display of anger from these strange alien devils.

As the brave little old women missionaries and the sturdy young Gospel preachers declared the love of God, and received a welcome fit for traitors; Jonathan Edwards and the Carnival Barker broke away from the missionaries, and headed straight into the deepest, darkest, most violent section of the village.

"If they won't accept the love of God, perhaps they'll enjoy Hell and Judgment," the Carnival Barker laughed.

Jonathan Edwards was always ready to share that message. In another time and place, he had preached America's most famous sermon in a church in Enfield, CT. On July 8th, 1741 the First Great Awakening was set off as people clawed at the pillars of the church crying out for mercy.

The missionary marchers continued their walk through the village, and encountered further mocking, cursing, and spitting. Meanwhile the Carnival Barker set himself on a small ledge next to the fountain in the village square. He gathered the attention of a crowd of cruel monsters, scantily clad witches, dark warlocks, voluptuous bloody vampires, and strange indescribable demons. The Carnival Barker told a story from the history of his world. It was a story of the great preacher, with a message about the fires of Hell. It was a story of churchgoers writhing on the floor in terror and clawing at the pillars of the church in Enfield, Connecticut, and of the resulting religious awakening. Monsters and Vampires stood enchanted by the magic of the Carnival Barker from another world, as he asked for their participation.

"We will be hearing from this famous ancient preacher, and his most famous message, 'Sinners in the Hands of an Angry God', and I need your help." The Carnival Barker pleaded with the crowd.

"Witches and Vampires, when you hear the word God, say 'Amen!'" and the Witches and Vampires captured by his mystical power shouted "Amen!"

"Monsters and demons, when you hear the word 'Hell' shout "Save us!''" and the hypnotized monsters and the demons cried "Save us!"

Jonathan Edwards stepped up to the fountain ledge. Being desperately far-sighted he adjusted his small reading glasses on his nose, and held his sermon notes high.

"There is no want in the power of God…"

"Amen!" shouted the Witches and Vampires.

Jonathan Edwards continued, "to cast wicked men into Hell."

"Save us!" the monsters and the demons growled joyously.

Jonathan Edwards and the Carnival Barker repeated their performance over and over throughout the night to the wandering crowds of monsters, and demons, and witches and vampires, who shouted and celebrated with them. They talked. They hugged. They laughed, and they discussed religion with one another.

Meanwhile 30 missionaries marched around the strange village speaking about the love of God to the venomous spit and angry curses of these same monstrous alien villagers.

My friend Rick MacDonald was Jonathan Edwards, and I was the Carnival Barker. The uncomfortable missionaries were a group of 30 Evangelical Christians performing a little "March for Jesus" through the city on October 31st, 1997. The strange little village is Salem, Massachusetts, and the crowds of sexy Witches, dark demons, and twisted monsters were the Halloween Night revelers, who came to celebrate the last and greatest night of a month-long festival. The spitting, the cursing, the tempting, and the mocking were exactly that: crowds of costumed people spitting, cursing, tempting, and mocking the Christian evangelists marching through the city. Rick and I followed the little parade, and before their first step out of the church doors, we knew this "March for Jesus" was going to be a bad idea.

As the group of evangelists traveled throughout the city, the clash of cultures could not have been more evident. A celebration of costumed people was faced with a small march of normally dressed church people singing church songs, and carrying banners with sayings like, "His Banner over me is Love" and "Lift Jesus High." The face of Evangelical religion had been assaulting Salem every Halloween for years, typically with bullhorn threats of Hell, and rebukes for celebrating the darkness of the Halloween season. Yet, this quaint little parade celebrating Jesus did not look any different to the crowds than the bullhorn toting, fire-and-brimstone-screaming preachers, and evoked frustration and anger.

Rick and I, on the other hand were costumed and armed with an historical vignette, and on that night I learned that a message is far more than the words that bear it. There is an unspoken language in carnival culture. It is found in music and in dance, in art and in costuming as the art upon the body, in food and in drink, in participation and interactive dialogue, in sharing and in learning about one another.

This was the interesting thing about that Halloween night: Those who talked about love were rejected, and those who talked about Hell created a party and made friends. Halloween is a wild inversion in a strange world, and how we approach the day just might be a model for how we approach the whole of society around us.

The Pastor in Witch City

June 1999, I rolled into town with a moving van, joined by a friend with his moving van. Two families were in the process of relocating 3,000 miles across the US to begin a church in Salem, Massachusetts. Jeff and his brother Bill, and my thirteen-year-old son – Elijah and I, arrived in the small city, which would become home for the next 19 years. The rest of the members of the family would join us a few weeks later. But, on arrival, it already felt like home to me.

Many Christians I knew described my move to Salem as, "Going into the gates of Hell." Their description was a bit overly dramatic, but it was not an uncommon feeling among Evangelical Christians in 1999.

I, on the other hand, felt like I was coming home. There was nothing homelike about Salem for a man who spent his entire life in Southern California, with most of that time being within short striking distance to some of the world's greatest beaches. Salem had weather. It had harsh winters and muggy summers. It had an extremely short but explosive spring, and stunningly colorful autumn. I came from a land with four seasons we jokingly described as "earthquake, fire, flood and riot." I also came from a place a guy could go down to the beach with his boards year round. I arrived in a place where the waves were only decent for surfing in the middle of the winter, and a guy had to crunch across the snow to paddle out into the surf.

People in New England are typically different than those born in California as well. There is a distinct personality trait common to New Englanders, especially those near Boston, which was wildly different than my Southern California chilled-out beach-dude casualness. On the North Shore of Boston people were quick, to the point, and in your face. This Boston area temperament is perceived as brash and aggressive. On some occasions outsiders see as refreshingly honest and straightforward. Whatever it was, it was a different way of life for me. People spoke to me at uncomfortable distances, like inches from my face, instead of at arm's length.

Somehow, in the midst of these differences, I felt more at home than I did back in California. For months after arriving, I would cross the border of the city as I drove in and out of town, and say out loud to myself as I passed the "Salem" sign, "Yes, this is my city!" I was excited to live there, even while others described Salem as "the gates of Hell." I was in love with Salem, Massachusetts.

Isn't this the heart of mission? That we love where we are, and whom we meet? That we find silver linings in the clouds of unfamiliarity and difference? The heart that seeks for the God Who is already making Himself known in the cultures of our world is the heart that is found in the missionary traveling across the seas to reach unknown lands. This same heart ought to be found in every Christian who looks into their neighborhood, and in every pastor who goes to work in a new setting. The places and times we live in are there for us to love in the same way that God loves them.

Within my first couple weeks in Salem, I wandered into a small basement office beneath a gift shop on Washington Street. This was the home of the Haunted Happenings Committee. They were in charge of organizing and promoting the 31 days of Halloween, which Salem calls "Haunted Happenings".

Three people feverishly took calls, made calls, and worked on flow charts and maps of the city. Between half a million and a million people would be pouring into the city in less than four months, and these three people had to prepare for the month-long event. They appeared overworked, and under pressure.

I introduced myself, "Hi, I'm Phil Wyman, and I'm a new pastor in town."

The three people stopped what they were doing, and looked at me. The woman I was talking to raised her eyebrows.

"I wanted to see if there was anything I could do to help with Halloween."

The eyebrows raised a little higher.

"I know there have been some problems in the past with Christian Churches and Halloween, and we wanted to help change that."

The eyebrows didn't move. She wasn't convinced, and neither were the other two in the room.

"Is there anything we can do to help?"

There was a pause, some blinking, then…

"We've had quite a bit of trouble with churches during Halloween."

"I know that some Christians have been antagonistic toward the city, and every year preachers bring their bullhorns, and yell at people on the streets, and pass out tracts that become trash. We want to teach people how to behave differently."

The eyebrows dropped a little, but not enough to show confidence in me.

"We'd like to help create the wonderful family-friendly atmosphere in Salem. What kind of help could you use?" I asked again.

Perhaps because they were simply too busy, or perhaps because I looked determined to get involved, she simply said, "I don't know. What would you like to do?"

Now, that is the one thing you don't want to say to me, if you don't want me involved, because I have at least one crazy idea every minute.

The underlying tension between the city of Salem, the Witches, and the Christians had been an ongoing struggle for a number of years, but in the mid 90's it was exacerbated by a Christian TV personality who blew into to town with the goal of making a name for himself as a radical evangelist.

Jeff Fenholt, who proclaimed he was an ex-singer for the band Black Sabbath (somehow Black Sabbath didn't remember him singing with them) arrived in Salem in June, 1992 with a former Witch by the name of Eric Pryor, who similarly had tall tales like Fenholt. Pryor declared himself to be a former leader of a large Pagan group. However, his stories turned out to be self-promotional exaggerations. During their brief encounter with Salem, they caused trouble while pretending to accomplish great things in the name of "spiritual warfare". They left the primarily Catholic city with the opinion that Evangelical Christians were a cult. This opinion had already been set in place by the street preaching and antics of a hyper-Pentecostal church, which had experienced some scandals, and had closed a few years before we arrived. Jeff and Eric, and a former local church had left a bad taste in the mouths of the police, the city officials, the Witches, and many of the Christians. I came into town in the smoke of their burning coattails. Their memory made my attempts at trying to be involved with Halloween more difficult. The city officials and event organizers were afraid of what churches might do during the holiday.

Over the next three months, we prepared for October. Our church had only a handful of people, because we had just arrived in town. What we didn't realize was that we were already falling into the center of Salem's Halloween experience.

The first thing we bought for the church was a decent sound system: not a small system for indoor meetings with small groups, but a sound system, which could, as I described it, "Pound the park." I had already noticed that the city did not have a good sound system for its events. A decent sound system would allow us to volunteer our services to run sound for those hard to hear city events. It also allowed us to think bigger about the Halloween events we could create in the city. This act of buying a decent sound system was part of a simple "find a need and fill it" plan. The city had a need. We wanted to provide the solution.

With the new sound system, we put in a request to the city to hold live music on the streets of Salem each weekend of the month. Along with the live music, we added a booth to serve hot cocoa, and a tent for "Psalm Readings."

After a number of meetings with the licensing board, I discovered that, not only were we allowed to set up in downtown Salem all four weekends of October, but they also gave us an entire square in front of the Old Town Hall.

I began dividing the verses of the Psalms into passages that talked about love, life, the heart, and the mind. These categories corresponded to the love line, life line, heart line, and head line used by Palm Readers, and this was our humorous way of riffing off Salem's Palm Reader experience, and playing with the reference to offer something from the Bible. I thought this might be a creative way to interest people in the Word of God, but I was not prepared for what was about to happen.

Someone heard about what we were doing and brought piles of lumber and helped build a crazy looking stage on the back of the Old Town Hall. Another church offered to make hot cocoa to give away. We set up a Psalm Reading booth, and I booked bands every afternoon and evening on the weekends.

We had created a party within the greater party, and our goal was to make our party the party to be at. Young Christian bands playing Ska, and Hardcore Metal banged away through the night, and solo musicians from Gordon College and the surrounding area joined us. Hot cocoa was being served for free at a pace we couldn't keep up with on the chilly New England evenings. Most surprising to us, people stood in line for free Psalm Readings.

We had a handful of volunteers for the Psalm Readings that first year. I trained them to sit across the table from people as they entered the tent, and introduce the "reading" by taking their open hand – palm upwards, and saying, "If you were to go to a Palm Reader, they would look at these lines on your hand: the head line, the heart line, the life line and the love line and see your past and your future in these lines, but we are doing something different here. We believe all these topics have been addressed by ancient mystics and prophets who spoke to these issues long ago. We do believe that your life is written in your hands, but it is in the daily actions you take to follow these ancient words of wisdom."

The person working as a Psalm Reader would then present a page with a scripture from the Psalms correlating to one of the four topics and read it out loud and then speak about its application to life, and discuss the verse with the participants. People not only enjoyed the experience, but because it was one of the only free events in a city filled with professional Palm Readers, Psychics, and Tarot Readers; they returned with their friends. Soon people were standing in line for over an hour for the experience.

Quickly we discovered that people could not read the sign that said "Free Psalm Readings". Because the mind of the Salem tourist is prepared for Psychics and Tarot Readers and the like, everyone sees the words "Free P-A-L-M Readings." After a couple days of providing Free Psalm Readings, I had to make signs with a picture of an open Bible, and the letter "S" in "Psalm" in red and hovering above the word with a little arrow pointing to it. Even with this precaution, those monitoring the lines would remind people that this would be a P-S-A-L-M reading and NOT a P-A-L-M Reading. Still people would sit down at the table in the tent and hold out their hands waiting for a Palm Reading. Despite giving scripture readings instead of Palm Readings, most people appeared pleased with the experience, and as this event repeated itself over the years, the same people would return each year for more.

In that first year, the defining moment occurred when the head of the Licensing Board, a retired police captain, stood in front of the makeshift stage while a young screaming Hardcore band was playing. I nervously watched Harold as he looked on rather stoically. He scanned the square with the pounding metal music, bouncing youth, people sipping hot cocoa, and others standing in line at the Psalm Reading tent. When the song ended, and we could actually hear each other well enough to hold a conversation, he said, "You run a class act here. Good job."

That was our official seal of approval from the city, and the beginning of years of missional engagement on the streets of Salem each Haunted Happenings season.

In that same year, we joined the Haunted Happenings Committee for a Children's Day on the Salem Common. This was an event sponsored by Domino's Pizza. It was designed as an event for the local children from ages four to twelve. We arrived with a tent to create a story-telling booth. We brought our sound system, and prepared to set up on the edge of the event. The city owned sound system that the event was expecting did not arrive, and our tent was better than the one they had for the main events, so I offered our tent and sound system for the event to use. It messed up our own plans, but that morning, we provided the main tent and the sound system, and instead of telling our stories to a handful of children at a time, we told our stories to the entire festival three times that day. This began a fourteen-year run of helping provide the primary local Children's Day event for the Halloween season in Salem.

The first year had provided the basic framework for the next years of involvement with the city of Salem during its massive October tourist season. We would provide free music on the streets each year. For many years, we would give away thousands of free cups of hot cocoa. We would involve ourselves with the local Children's Day event. And, all these things would allow us to create an environment to provide free spiritual advice in creative ways that people enjoyed receiving.

Over the years, this basic framework would morph into a variety of creative expressions, and sometimes be challenged by the politics of the city, or the commercialism of the holiday, but it would remain intact for many years.

Psalm Readings were expanded to include simple things like Healing Prayers. Charismatic and Pentecostal Christians would offer "Spiritual Readings", that provided Christians the opportunity to speak graciously and prophetically into people's lives. Others offered Dream Interpretation, which became one of the most popular experiences we provided.

A Confessional Booth was added for a few years. Christians dressed as monks offered free confessions, but taking a cue from Donald Miller's book Blue Like Jazz, we confessed the sins of the church to people rather than hearing the confession of their sins.

Each of these experiences touched the visiting public in different ways, and without fail we watched people stand in line for the experiences year after year.

From the first year in Salem, I had my eye on moving the music stage, hot cocoa booth, and Psalm Reading tents to a busier location on Essex Street. A square with a fountain was a central gathering point over the weekends, but nothing was occurring in that location. Late on Halloween night, it became an empty square filled with people looking for something to do. Large gatherings of people – late at night – many of them drunk or high with nothing to do is a dangerous thing in a festival setting. Seeing this problem, I suggested placing the stage in the fountain. For a couple years I made this suggestion, and no one saw the benefit, until on our fourth year in Salem, the Police Chief, the licensing board chairman, the Fire Chief, and the Haunted Happenings event coordinator were all sitting in a planning meeting discussing the problem of the fountain square. I quietly suggested to the Police Chief that we could place the stage in the fountain to help monitor the area each weekend through the month. Though I had suggested this in previous years, a light seemed to turn on in his head, and he suggested the idea to the rest of the city leaders in the room. Suddenly, our stage and the accompanying tents were in the best location in Salem for Halloween foot traffic.

Twenty Years of Outreach

After almost twenty years of mission on the streets of Salem each October, we have had thousands of people come to help us. Teams from California, Texas, North Carolina, New Hampshire, Maine, and the UK have joined nearby Massachusetts Christians to be a part of this vibrant outreach event. Some of these teams have gone on to take the lessons they've learned in Salem and apply them in festival settings around the US and the UK. The effect of Halloween in Salem is having worldwide ramifications. People are being touched by a gracious and fun expression of Christianity, and Christians are learning to take this same pattern of outreach to places typically antagonistic to a missional Christian presence.

The Betrayal of Superstition

Could it be that the biggest hindrance we have to participation in Halloween is superstition? That is the question of this chapter.

Superstition is a betrayer. It is a double-edged sword with no hilt. It cuts the hand that wields it.

Superstition causes people to attribute power to things that are powerless, or assume evil intent or special blessings to things that are inherently ambivalent. The superstitious person may feel empowered by the so-called knowledge they believe they hold, or they may be fearful and retreat in seclusion. The power of superstition holds people under its influence and causes them to behave in strange ways. Superstition is like a bad relationship. One moment it feels exciting, perhaps even adventurous, but the person under its spell is forced to dance to its tune. People remain locked up in their homes, because of the cruel power of superstition; or behave wildly in public, because superstition pulls their strings like a puppet master playing with the puppet.

If you are afraid to leave your home because it is a dangerous world, Saint Benedict will keep you from harm. You can place his medallion around your neck. The composer, Arnold Schoenberg, was terrified of the number 13, and refused to use that number in his work. So, instead of 13 between measures 12 and 14 it would be labeled 12a. Halloween, like Friday the 13th, is one of those days, which brings out the superstitions in people.

In the first few years of pastoring in Salem, six of us from our small church in Salem attended our denomination's national conference in Philadelphia. During a gathering of other pastors and church leaders from New England, we sat at a table with a group from a small church in Rhode Island. As we got to know one another, the topic of Halloween in Salem came up, because, after all, Salem is famous for both Witches and Halloween and people want to know about it. We described our interaction with the city and its many visitors during Halloween. We talked about the ministry opportunities we had experienced among thousands of people. At this news, the pastor of the church in Rhode Island held her fingers up to her lips in the sign of a cross, scrunched up her face, and hissed at us. After that, she turned away, and treated us as though we had some contagious disease.

That interaction became a weird story we laughed about for years, and it highlights the betraying power of superstition. The pastor from Rhode Island felt empowered by her superstitious belief that Halloween was an inherently evil day, and she acted like a horror movie exorcist towards us. Because we were participating in city events during Halloween, we apparently were practitioners of evil in her eyes. Her peculiar belief empowered her to act aggressively, but she ended up looking like a character in a Comedy Horror spoof.

Halloween is a day that focuses upon many of our cultures strange superstitions. Astrology and Tarot become big business during Halloween. People are afraid of evil spirits and ghosts, and talk about it on this day, and at midnight they become fearful, because the veil between the unseen world and our world is supposedly at its thinnest.

Now, I will admit to a certain degree of superstition as defined by the radical materialist atheist. I believe in a God that loves me, and I believe that pleasing God is the right thing to do. I believe that God is involved with our world, and that supernatural things can happen. Yes, He is my invisible Friend. I also believe in angels and devils, but I am extremely hesitant to attribute small daily actions or even cataclysmic world events to the acts of God or the devil.

I do not pay attention to horoscopes, whether in the newspaper, or in complex charts laid out by experienced astrologers. When someone asks me my sign, I tell them I am a Scorpio, and I typically keep it to myself that it doesn't mean anything to me.

Astrology is one of the superstitious things common to our culture, which is usually harmless, and not worth my attention, but on occasion, it is a superstition that cripples people.

I do not see one location on earth as more spiritual than another. I do not attribute more holiness to one day over another. Similarly, I do not believe one location is more wicked than another, or one day more evil than another. People may perform evil acts, and our memories of those acts can make times and places feel creepy, or remind us of difficult times we desire to forget. Decay and rot cause old buildings to look and sound haunted and mysterious, but I am not moved by the fear of supernatural activity emanating from them.

Years ago, I worked in a boy's home in Salem. It was said that the third floor of the massive early 1800's house was haunted. The man who worked the overnight shift regularly told the story of a supposed ghost lady who haunted the building, and said that if he ever saw the ghost, he would simply run away and head home leaving the kids to themselves. I worked his shift one night, and he asked what I would do if I saw the ghost.

I jokingly responded, "I'm not afraid of ghosts. They're afraid of me."

This is exactly how I feel about Halloween. I'm not afraid of Halloween, but it should be afraid of me, because I have come like Martin Luther nailing his 95 theses to its door.

The Bible warns against treating one day as better than another in some sort of superstitious manner. It also highlights how we should respond to those who are judgmental about our own dealings with certain days and seasons.

> *"Therefore do not let anyone judge you by what you eat or drink, or with regard to a religious festival, a New Moon celebration or a Sabbath day. These are a shadow of the things that were to come; the reality, however, is found in Christ." (Colossians 2:16-17)*

So, whether you participate in the activities of a holiday, or ignore that holiday, let no one judge you. Don't allow someone to evaluate your spirituality on the basis of your diet, or involvement with the seasons on the calendar of the year.

This brings us to the real point of this chapter: If you believe that one day is inherently more special than another in some mystical way, you may be superstitious. If you believe that one day is inherently more evil than another day in some mystical way, you may also be superstitious.

You have freedom to respond to days like Halloween in whatever way you choose. I choose to treat every day the same, and attribute nothing special to that day except what happens on it, and if I can help make good things happen, it becomes a great day.

I suppose I do have a special relationship with Halloween, but it is not because the day is special. I have a special relationship with Halloween, because other people are involved with it in large numbers.

They are looking to create family moments, and to find experiences to remember.

I do not celebrate Halloween because it is such a special day to me. Instead I participate in Halloween in order to develop relationships with other people who are celebrating Halloween, and to be a witness to them about God's love. My engagement with Halloween is missional. I treat Halloween like every other day of the year, I seek to redeem the day and make it the Lord's Day.

Of course, Halloween is also Reformation Day, and the eve of All Saint's Day, so redeeming the day should be a no-brainer for Christians. It is what we have called, "All Hallows Eve." If there is an original Christian superstition to Halloween, it is the belief that it is a holy day.

Community and Halloween

My favorite Christmas song is from a musician who calls himself, "a heathen and a pagan" at the end of his song. "The Rebel Jesus" by Jackson Browne walks through the activities of an American Christmas. We give gifts to our relatives, and "if the generosity should seize us", we will put a little aside for the poor. This song highlights the struggle we have to maintain faithful celebration of religious holydays.

I am going to put myself out in front of the firing squad, and stand at the post. I will even tie the blindfold over my eyes. What I am going to say next is the equivalent of doing just that. But, there's no use in mincing words, so here we go:

I think Halloween just might be the most Christian holiday in America.

I can hear a voice calling out, "Ready…Aim…" but don't shout the command, "Fire!" just yet, not at least until you've heard me out.

The next two chapters are focused upon this crazy idea. In this chapter, I will look at social dynamics that make Halloween a positive experience for many people. Weirdly, churches are trying to create these same dynamics every Sunday and don't realize it. In the next chapter, I will highlight the biblical themes that are found in Halloween celebrations.

First, let's look at a few of the American holidays with clear Christian roots: Easter and the day of Christ's resurrection, Christmas and the day of Christ's birth, and Thanksgiving with its gratefulness to God for the embryonic roots of the United States of America and for His providence over our lives.

Yes, Easter is the day of the resurrection of Christ, and as Christians, we remember what we understand to be the most amazing moment in world history. On that day, Christians typically get dressed up a little fancier than we do on other days of the year. We go to church to "celebrate" the resurrection of Christ from the dead. Those from more liturgical traditions may attend a Good Friday service, and if you are especially zealous, you might add Maundy Thursday. If you have been extra devoted, you might have had ashes daubed on your forehead forty-something days before Easter and fasted in a variety of ways through Lent. Most of this happens as a reminder to Christians about the things we hold most dear, and it is a deep, abiding testament about the power of Christ and His resurrection.

Of course, there is the other side to Easter. We see it in every grocery store as the holiday approaches. It is a day of flowers, chocolate, Easter Egg Hunts, and bunnies. This is what much of America sees and celebrates each Easter as it comes around.

There are people who try to attach Easter day to an ancient pagan celebration of Ishtar, a Babylonian fertility goddess, or Ostara, a pagan Germanic goddess of the spring, but I have little interest in these ideas that seem to amount to something like ancient conspiracy theories. I am happy enough with the Christian holiday of Easter as it is.

Christmas marks the birth of Christ for us. Of course, most of us realize that this was probably not the actual day of Christ's birth, and one can find all sorts of debate about the pagan origin of Christmas Trees, or the date given for His birth being related to the Roman Saturnalia celebration occurring around the winter solstice. I am not particularly interested in these supposed reasons for avoiding Christmas either. Christmas has enough problems by itself to make me want to avoid it most years.

Christmas is most certainly one of the high holy days of the church, but it has been absconded by capitalism over the last 100+ years. Long before the day arrives, the Christmas advertisements appear in the stores with amazing aggression. We are encouraged to "give to our relations", as Jackson Browne sings. Maybe, if we are feeling especially spiritual or generous, we will become socially aware by giving something to the poor. More radical thinkers will help create meals for the homeless, or invite people who have no families to their homes. But on the whole, Christmas is a day of celebration with family and maybe a few friends. In fact, we often fight over what part of the family we have to visit each Christmas. It is a day of giving to those we already love, and sometimes we have a hard time loving them. Our real hope is to take a rest from the stresses of this messy world, and our sometimes messy lives.

Thanksgiving is a day much like Christmas. Instead of remembering the birth of Christ, Americans try to remember the Pilgrims, whose landing at Plymouth and first year of living in the New World was the tiny beginnings of the birth of our nation. Although to be honest, most of us won't mention the pilgrims on that day. This too, is fraught with the same capitalistic tendencies as Christmas, and with the same relational tensions. It is a gastronomical variation of the gift giving of the Christmas season. It is one of the world's great feast days, but it too has become insular. It is simply a family day off for most people. Well, except for the cook, who works longer and harder than most other days of the year.

Problematically, each of the above holidays carries a load of capitalistic pressure. Our ability to celebrate these holidays in the traditional American manner directly corresponds to how much money we are able to spend. If you are poor, you either become poorer and deeper in debt to participate, or you have to buck the system in order to celebrate these holidays meaningfully.

So this brings us to Halloween. I am not going to suggest that Halloween is free from the bondage to commercial pressure, but I will suggest that it inherently carries a freedom and rebellion against the system that is still evident in the manner in which our nation celebrates it.

Don't shout, "Fire!" to the firing squad just yet. Consider these things about Halloween first:

Halloween is Intergenerational

In the mid-60's, when I was little, parents and children went out together trick-or-treating. When the children got a little older – perhaps eight or nine years old, they were allowed to go out with their friends without the parents. Maybe an older brother or sister would tag along. In the days when people still trusted their neighbors, the kids would go out without adults, and the whole neighborhood watched everyone's kids as they traveled from candy stop to candy stop. The whole neighborhood was a series of candy stores.

Today, there may be less trust, but a competing thing has occurred to counterbalance the lack of trust in our society, and continue Halloween's popularity; people still remember Halloween as their favorite holiday. They want to recreate the wild fun, and continue to celebrate that day in their adulthood. They still dress up in crazy costumes and throw silly parties with themes of horror movies or historical events. Halloween is no longer a holiday for the children. It is an event for every age.

In Salem, people who love Halloween come into the city on the weekends through the entire month. They come in costume and it doesn't have to be Halloween day for them to get dressed up. Over the last few years (the printing of this book is 2018), the amount of money and time people put into their costuming appears to have grown. Many of the visitors in costume are now better dressed than the street performers who are busking over the long Halloween season. The effort adults are putting into costuming for Halloween is evidence of the growth of the holiday. It has expanded beyond being an event for the kids to dress up, run around the neighborhood, and collect candy. Parents throw parties. Students in college throw parties. Taverns, pubs, and clubs are packed to capacity with Halloween events. Haunted Houses are found in every region of the country. Neighborhoods are inundated with gangs of little monsters roaming the streets, and garages are turned into haunted houses for the older kids, and fun rooms for the little kids.

While this is happening, American society is becoming increasingly segregated into age brackets. Youth and adults do not spend the time together they once did. Retirees are purchasing homes behind gated communities. The elderly are placed into care facilities, and many of them are seldom visited. Children are bracketed into appropriate age groups, and we assume that a healthy social upbringing is one where they spend the preponderance of their time with friends their own age.

Halloween has from the beginning been a family affair. It battles against the tendency to segregate people into age groups. Old and young alike gather for the party that is Halloween. Who would have thought that Halloween allows us the experience respecting our elders:

> *"Stand up in the presence of the aged, show respect for the elderly and revere your God. I am the Lord." (Leviticus 19:32)*

Halloween is an Open Community Event

Once a year, people buy lots of candy. They ready their homes for neighbors and strangers alike, and prepare a celebratory greeting. Children knock on their doors, and in anticipation the doors are answered. The residents discover surprising things. Princesses, cowboys, little monsters, funny animals, policemen, and superheroes are at the door. Sometimes even stranger things will arrive at the doorstep. There are peculiar creatures like walking talking vacuum cleaners or ketchup bottles. Of course, witches and little devils are also featured stars in the lineup of costumed children.

Perhaps, the most amazing thing about Halloween is the fact that so many people open their doors to a public invasion for this one day each year.

Can you name another day that allows people the freedom to dress up strange and dress their children even stranger, go the neighbor's house, knock on the door, shout at them when they open the door, and have them tell you how wonderful you all look and give you a gift for harassing them? No, of course you can't think of a day with as much silly community celebration and openness as Halloween. The fact that we live in a culture that celebrates such kookiness and expressive freedom, during a season of mistrust such as we have today is remarkable. The rest of the year, we drag ourselves out of bed, take a shower, eat a hurried (and usually unhealthy) breakfast, and run off to work. When we return from work, we have children's schedules to deal with, and errands to run. We ignore our neighbors, and pass strangers without a smile or nod. We may try to keep the house clean, and maybe once a week, we go do something we enjoy in the evening. Well, we'll go out to do something we enjoy, if we haven't fallen on the couch in front of the episodes of The Walking Dead, or The Big Bang Theory.

And, that is the struggle within our culture right now. We are overworked, and often underpaid for that work. We feel harassed by life, and we have isolated ourselves in our tiredness, and in our fear about the societal tensions in our culture.

Holidays promise to offer a break from these tensions. Unfortunately, some of the holidays, like Christmas, increase the pressure by encouraging debt and family dissonance. Strangely, Halloween is a wild, happy break for many people. Depending on the statistics you read, it may be the 2nd largest holiday of the year in the United States. And, it is a party in the neighborhood. It is an open invitation to people beyond our typical circles of influence.

Yes, as strange as it may sound, Halloween provides the opportunity to "love your neighbor." It is one of the best days in the year for people to live in open community.

Examples of Intergenerational Community

In Salem, Massachusetts, the first Thursday of October is the official Halloween kick-off. The Haunted Happenings Parade, run by the Chamber of Commerce brings the entire city together. The grade schools march in the parade with the children dressed in themed costumes. Local High School bands march. Politicians running and gunning for election in November enter the parade. The local clubs and businesses, and circles of friends enter the parade with floats and live music or lawn chair brigades. The Ghost Busters arrive – both the old and the new version. Typically someone will be riding a hearse dressed as a skeleton or the Grim Reaper.

And, of course, the local Witches march together in solidarity as well. Just like everyone else, the Witches in Salem are simply part of the community. They march in their ceremonial garb, and wave at the crowd, and give away candy to the kids, and NO, no one has ever been poisoned by the candy.

During our first year in Salem, we put together a small band for the parade, rode on the back of a flatbed truck, and played a reggae song through the parade. Since it was our first year in the city, we simply let people know we were a new Christian church, played a short tune about the "Word of God", and let people know who we were. Our goals were simple: We wanted people to know that we were simple Bible believing Christians, and that we were not afraid to be a part of the month-long Halloween season. In fact, we were letting people know that we were interested in being a creative part of the community events surrounding Halloween, and the parade was only the beginning of our first year doing Halloween in Salem

Just a few months prior to this parade, I had walked into the basement office of the Haunted Happenings committee on Washington Street.

I had told the Haunted Happenings Committee, that I understood churches had caused problems in the past, and I also promised to do two things: 1) to teach Christians how to behave properly during Halloween, and, 2) to help create a "family friendly" atmosphere.

I was familiar with the recent history of Halloween in Salem. Over the years, Christians had picketed the parade, and preached on the streets with bullhorns and protest signs warning people about Hell and Judgment. Preachers passed out Gospel tracts like sales brochures in the carnival, and the tracts simply became trash on the streets. I told them that these were the things we would avoid. I also knew that the term "family friendly" was of critical importance to the city of Salem, and we wanted to help make that a reality as much as we could.

That first year, we proved that what we said and what we did was going to be the same thing, and we were able to do that without compromising our values and our beliefs.

Halloween is a massive community event in the city of Salem. Some businesses live and die off the money that comes in from Halloween. Locals get involved and create this family friendly community event that also happens to invite the whole world into its celebration. The things we did that first year convinced Salem locals that our little church was a positive intergenerational family-friendly community force in our city.

Jeff's Good Name

Jeff and Diane Menasco joined us in the wild adventure of moving across the United States to start the church in Salem, Massachusetts. In that first year, Jeff kept reminding me that we had a fairly simple mission: 1) we were there to bless the city in whatever manner we could find to do so, and 2) that having a good name was more important than experiencing any outward successes.

The first point was birthed from our reading of church growth and evangelism material. I was not a fan of the large mass of "church growth" literature that came out in the 80's. It often focused upon the corporate structure and business side of running a church, and emphasized growth in numbers, but people like Ed Silvoso, who told a room full of pastors and their wives that I was going to become a "pastor to the witches, like Daniel was in Babylon", focused upon more practical things like blessing our cities, and the people in them.

The second point came from Proverbs 22:1, "A good name is more desirable than great riches." This Bible verse became a road sign for our actions. Having a good reputation based on serving the community was of greater value than monetary or numerical success. Jeff's regular reminder of these simple points helped keep our little group on the narrow track of blessing the community. In our strange case, being involved in Halloween was part of blessing the city.

These community aspects of Halloween can become a basis to bless our communities. But with this point, we have only begun to scratch the surface of this topic of the inherent spiritual and community nature of Halloween. In the next chapter, I plan to blow your mind. I will show how Halloween, is in many ways, downright biblical.

The Intrinsic Biblical Values of Halloween

I am sure you are still asking yourself what possessed me to believe that Halloween just might be the most Christian holiday of the year. In fact, you may be using the word "possessed" in its most biblical sense, and you are preparing to call an exorcist to come and deliver me from this devilish belief.

Saying that Halloween holds inherent biblical values may seem like a crazy contradiction. Worse than a contradiction, it may seem insane or demonic. How can Halloween have any intrinsic biblical values?! After all, Halloween is filled with motifs of horror movies, witches, and a whole host of other dark things like demons, occult magic, monsters and death. But, if we take a moment to consider these themes that are celebrated on the 31st of October, (or in my case, the entire month of October); we will see that these are the things that the church is already discussing throughout the year. Halloween brings these themes out into the square of public discourse like no other day.

Follow me for a short journey through the wild and strange topics that are common themes of every Halloween. I plan to show that these are themes we find, of all places, in the Bible. In fact, The Bible had these concepts long before Halloween was a thing, and I will show how Halloween is shredding on Biblical themes like a lead guitarist in a metal band.

Halloween and Spirits

Ghosts and the variety of disembodied spirits that fill the pages and the screens of horror and fantasy tales are some of the most common Halloween themes. The easiest, and perhaps most familiar Halloween costume is the sheet over the head with eyeholes cut into it. Who hasn't put a sheet over their head and made moaning noises, pretending to be a ghost, at some point in their lives?

With the growth of radical materialism and its denial of an unseen realm, the introduction of spirits into the discussion of everyday life is a breath of fresh air. It is in moments like these that the possibility exists that there is more to life than what we see, earn, acquire, and do each day. There is an invisible realm of possibilities, and responsibilities. This invisible realm is the realm of the Christian Church with its focus upon the spiritual realm – the place of God, and the Person of Jesus.

The fact that people put spiritual things out in the forefront of their celebrations makes Halloween an inherently spiritual holiday. Had we paid attention to the whispering of the Holy Ghost, we might have seen opportunities instead of warnings. Take note of these stories from the pages of the Bible with their reference to that realm of spirits: both good and evil.

> *"The Philistines assembled and came and set up camp at Shunem, while Saul gathered all Israel and set up camp at Gilboa. When Saul saw the Philistine army, he was afraid; terror filled his heart. 6 He inquired of the Lord, but the Lord did not answer him by dreams or Urim or prophets. Saul then said to his attendants, "Find me a woman who is a medium, so I may go and inquire of her."*
>
> *"There is one in Endor," they said.*
>
> *So Saul disguised himself, putting on other clothes, and at night he and two men went to the woman. "Consult a spirit for me," he said, "and bring up for me the one I name."*
>
> *But the woman said to him, "Surely you know what Saul has done. He has cut off the mediums and spiritists from the land. Why have you set a trap for my life to bring about my death?"*
>
> *Saul swore to her by the Lord, "As surely as the Lord lives, you will not be punished for this."*
>
> *Then the woman asked, "Whom shall I bring up for you?"*
>
> *"Bring up Samuel," he said.*
>
> *When the woman saw Samuel, she cried out at the top of her voice and said to Saul, "Why have you deceived me? You are Saul!"*
>
> *The king said to her, "Don't be afraid. What do you see?"*
>
> *The woman said, "I see a ghostly figure[a] coming up out of the earth."*
>
> *"What does he look like?" he asked.*

"An old man wearing a robe is coming up," she said.

Then Saul knew it was Samuel, and he bowed down and prostrated himself with his face to the ground.

Samuel said to Saul, "Why have you disturbed me by bringing me up?"

"I am in great distress," Saul said. "The Philistines are fighting against me, and God has departed from me. He no longer answers me, either by prophets or by dreams. So I have called on you to tell me what to do."

Samuel said, "Why do you consult me, now that the Lord has departed from you and become your enemy? The Lord has done what he predicted through me. The Lord has torn the kingdom out of your hands and given it to one of your neighbors—to David. Because you did not obey the Lord or carry out his fierce wrath against the Amalekites, the Lord has done this to you today. The Lord will deliver both Israel and you into the hands of the Philistines, and tomorrow you and your sons will be with me. The Lord will also give the army of Israel into the hands of the Philistines."

Immediately Saul fell full length on the ground, filled with fear because of Samuel's words. His strength was gone, for he had eaten nothing all that day and all that night." (I Samuel 28:4-20)

"When the day of Pentecost came, they were all together in one place. Suddenly a sound like the blowing of a violent wind came from heaven and filled the whole house where they were sitting. They saw what seemed to be tongues of fire that separated and came to rest on each of them. All of them were filled with the Holy Spirit and began to speak in other tongues as the Spirit enabled them." (Acts 2:1-4)

Halloween and the Supernatural

Christianity is accused of being out of touch, because of its focus upon otherworldly things. During Halloween, these are suddenly the topics of intense interest and wild celebration. In the aggressive "new atheist" movement, all things supernatural are rejected, and in fact, are treated as infantile obsessions. Science has become the new savior, and all things magical and miraculous are rejected as fairy tales. Halloween has given us a reprieve from this sterile material world of numbers and animal instincts. It poetically forces the supernatural back upon us. Movies with themes of magical forces, both good and evil, are timed for release in October to correspond with the coming of Halloween. People dress up in the costumes of superheroes, witches, and magical monsters of all sorts, and they live for a day as though they believe these things are real.

For the Christian, who believes that a miraculous world with a powerful God underlies everything we see, this day of celebration of the supernatural should be seen as an opportunity. These are the moments when people consider that there is something more to this world than what meets the eye, or is measurable by scales and scopes. Halloween is an opportunity to focus on supernatural issues and discuss them – even celebrate them – with the revelers around us. Everyone becomes mystical at Halloween. Everyone begins believing in magic again.

Horror movies have given us exorcists reciting scripture, and driving out devils by the power of God's word. Antichrist characters roam the earth and seek to initiate the apocalypse using their occult powers. The pages of the Gospels, the Book of Acts, and even the Book of Revelation seem to come to life each October, and we are reminded that weird things sometimes really do happen in this world.

Yet, the supernatural is not only dangerous and fearsome. It also shows itself in gentle ways. Like Glenda, the good witch in "The Wizard of OZ", magic comes with a smile and a blessing. Good witches, fairies, pixies, dwarves, elves, and wizards appear at this season alongside the demons and monsters. Characters like Gandalf, and Cinderella's Fairy God Mother arrive in costume at our doors. They are reminders that just because something is supernatural and powerful, it does not have to be destructive. These fantasy beings are typological images of the awesome power of a benevolent God. One moment they appear dangerous, but to those they love, they are both protectors and correctors. They bring healing, help, and guidance in time of need.

The Bible places supernatural events in front of our eyes every time we read it. Sometimes they are written as actual events, and at other times dark fearsome images from dreams or visions are used to tell stories, and relate truths. It reminds us that the material world should not be the sole focus of life. Consider how supernaturally wild these passages from the Bible are:

> *"The Lord said to Moses and Aaron, "When Pharaoh says to you, 'Perform a miracle,' then say to Aaron, 'Take your staff and throw it down before Pharaoh,' and it will become a snake.*

So Moses and Aaron went to Pharaoh and did just as the Lord commanded. Aaron threw his staff down in front of Pharaoh and his officials, and it became a snake. Pharaoh then summoned wise men and sorcerers, and the Egyptian magicians also did the same things by their secret arts: Each one threw down his staff and it became a snake. But Aaron's staff swallowed up their staffs. Yet Pharaoh's heart became hard and he would not listen to them, just as the Lord had said." (Exodus 7:8-13)

"Daniel said: "In my vision at night I looked, and there before me were the four winds of heaven churning up the great sea. Four great beasts, each different from the others, came up out of the sea.

The first was like a lion, and it had the wings of an eagle. I watched until its wings were torn off and it was lifted from the ground so that it stood on two feet like a human being, and the mind of a human was given to it.

And there before me was a second beast, which looked like a bear. It was raised up on one of its sides, and it had three ribs in its mouth between its teeth. It was told, 'Get up and eat your fill of flesh!'

After that, I looked, and there before me was another beast, one that looked like a leopard. And on its back it had four wings like those of a bird. This beast had four heads, and it was given authority to rule.

After that, in my vision at night I looked, and there before me was a fourth beast—terrifying and frightening and very powerful. It had large iron teeth; it crushed and devoured its victims and trampled underfoot whatever was left. It was different from all the former beasts, and it had ten horns." (Daniel 7:2-7)

"The disciples of the prophets said to Elisha, "The place where we're staying is too small for us. Let's go to the Jordan River. Each of us can get some logs and make a place for us to live there."

Elisha said, "Go ahead."

Then one of the disciples asked, "Won't you please come with us?"

Elisha answered, "I'll go."

So he went with them. They came to the Jordan River and began to cut down trees. As one of them was cutting down a tree, the ax head fell into the water. He cried out, "Oh no, master! It was borrowed!"

The man of God asked, "Where did it fall?" When he showed Elisha the place, Elisha cut off a piece of wood. He threw it into the water at that place and made the ax head float. Elisha said, "Pick it up." The disciple reached for it and picked it up." (II Kings 6:1-7)

"As he went along, he saw a man blind from birth. His disciples asked him, "Rabbi, who sinned, this man or his parents, that he was born blind?"

"Neither this man nor his parents sinned," said Jesus, "but this happened so that the works of God might be displayed in him. As long as it is day, we must do the works of him who sent me. Night is coming, when no one can work. While I am in the world, I am the light of the world."

After saying this, he spit on the ground, made some mud with the saliva, and put it on the man's eyes. "Go," he told him, "wash in the Pool of Siloam" (this word means "Sent"). So the man went and washed, and came home seeing." (John 9:1-7)

Halloween and Heaven and Hell

The contrasts of opposite and competing values like good and evil, and light and dark are part of the dramatic tension that makes Halloween a day of excitement. These contrasting opposites are part of the technique of tension and resolution found in classic fairy tales and great fiction. Heroes and villains, the cruel and the innocent face off in desperation and hope. Yet, there is an even more popular contrast that is seen in the celebration of Halloween.

Heaven and Hell is one of the most common couplings of opposites during Halloween. Halloween has taken one of the most controversial topics in the Bible, and made it a popular subject. Even though our society feels that the topic of Hell is a cruel and terrible thing, it gets celebrated at the end of each October. How weird is that? Weirder yet, how weird is it that most Christians have not made the connection that this just might be a good thing?

Movies like "Hellraiser", and "What Dreams May Come" have presented this topic in the realm of fantasy and horror, and captured public imagination.

Biblical references to Hell are extremely unpopular today. If they ever were popular is unlikely, but we may have come to a point when the topic is close to taboo. Halloween inverts this problem, and all of a sudden Hell is an exciting subject.

The following passages are not meant to be a theology on the topics of Heaven and Hell. They are simply highlighting the fact that the popular Halloween topic of Hell is a biblical topic, which Halloween has been using as a major motif throughout the rise of its popularity as a holiday. Consider how dramatic some of these Bible references are that deal with Heaven and Hell:

"If your hand causes you to stumble, cut it off. It is better for you to enter life maimed than with two hands

to go into hell, where the fire never goes out." (Mark 9:43)

"The time came when the beggar died and the angels carried him to Abraham's side. The rich man also died and was buried. In Hades, where he was in torment, he looked up and saw Abraham far away, with Lazarus by his side. So he called to him, 'Father Abraham, have pity on me and send Lazarus to dip the tip of his finger in water and cool my tongue, because I am in agony in this fire.' But Abraham replied, 'Son, remember that in your lifetime you received your good things, while Lazarus received bad things, but now he is comforted here and you are in agony.' " (Luke 16:22-26)

"They marched across the breadth of the earth and surrounded the camp of God's people, the city he loves. But fire came down from heaven and devoured them. And the devil, who deceived them, was thrown into the lake of burning sulfur, where the beast and the false prophet had been thrown. They will be tormented day and night for ever and ever." (Revelation 20:9-10)

Halloween and Good and Evil

With the contrast of good and evil, and dark and light as part of the storyline of Halloween, the struggle of truth itself is captured in these opposing values. Angels and devils, demons and priests, monsters and heroes, murderous villains and innocent survivors: These are the characters of the costuming, movies, and stories attached to the season.

But, just when the opportunity arrives for the church to uninhibitedly portray its beliefs and values in creative ways, it hides away in fear of being perceived as a participant in some occult practice. Yes, Halloween is a world of dark evils and miraculous interventions, but that evil is almost entirely expressed in drama and roleplaying. If you ask me, dark evil and miraculous intervention sounds like an overview of the Bible. When our culture finally focuses upon good and evil, and sees the tension of these opposing forces in the same way the Bible describes it, we ignore the moment and hope it will go away. Meanwhile our neighbors want to celebrate these themes. I could not have dreamed up a better cultural opportunity to be my biblical self in a postmodern world than Halloween, but trying to convince other Christians of this opportunity has not been easy.

This so-called occult holiday just might be the closest thing to a celebration of the real world truths Evangelical Christianity has ever seen in American culture. Halloween presents a world of black and white, of truth and lies, and good and evil. We can see the black-hatted bad guys and the white-hatted good guys; we can see the tormentors and the saviors as people play their respective parts in the game.

Halloween seems to focus on the competing forces of good and evil in much the same way as the Bible:

> *"The Lord God took the man and put him in the Garden of Eden to work it and take care of it. And the Lord God commanded the man, "You are free to eat from any tree in the garden; but you must not eat from the tree of the knowledge of good and evil, for when you eat from it you will certainly die."" (Genesis 2:15-17)*

> *"Woe to those who call evil good and good evil, who put darkness for light and light for darkness, who put bitter for sweet and sweet for bitter." (Isaiah 5:20)*

"Turn from evil and do good; then you will dwell in the land forever." (Psalm 37:27)

"The light shines in the darkness, and the darkness has not overcome it." (John 1:5)

Halloween and Death

Christianity is filled with life and death stories: the life and death of Christ, the options of choosing life in obedience to God, or death in choosing against Him. The Apostle Paul discusses what occurs following the death of each human, and Daniel and the Book of Revelation foresee the coming of deadly apocalyptic times. Life and death are found from the story of humanity's first encounter with God in the Garden of Eden to the last story of the coming of the New Jerusalem and eternal life in the last chapter of Revelation.

Halloween, known as the Day of the Dead in Mexico, faces the topic of death more completely than any other day in our culture. It seems strange to me that when our world begins to consider the issues of life and death, that the church becomes silent.

Today, the fairy tales we have been reading to our children have been expunged of the violent themes found in the original telling, but many of the old fairy tales are reappearing in their more gruesome original forms. Scholars like Maria Tatar from Harvard; and Dame Marina Warner, the President of Britain's Royal Society of Literature (2017) are helping us rethink the value of the fairy tales' and their original wildness. A movement rediscovering fairy tales that model the real and sometimes violent elements of life is happening. It is as though people are naturally predisposed to loving the gruesome stories of danger and death, with its wild hope, as we find them in the old fairy tales. Could Halloween simply be part of this revival of brutally honest themes of life and death?

There is certainly no question that Halloween fights against our attempt to tell gentler tales. It will not allow us to sanitize our stories for the sake of feeling more comfortable in a deadly world. Halloween reminds us that we cannot escape this world alive, and it does it with both horror and humor.

The denial of death seems like an American preoccupation, and unfortunately that preoccupation has infiltrated the church, which should be last bastion of holding to the truth. In fact, this preoccupation with denying death and aging has spawned scores of occupations. Plastic surgeons and pharmaceutical companies, the cosmetic and fashion industries, Hollywood and the music industry all celebrate youth, and do their best to ignore the coming of age and death. Halloween looks death in the face, and responds like the small group of people boarding up the house as Zombies are approaching in "Night of the Living Dead." As grotesque and fearful as death appears to us, at least it is honest. It reminds us of our temporary engagement with this earth, and makes us consider what might come after.

We live in a world of people shouting at each other like weightlifters at the gym, telling us we are strong and we can do anything. Halloween drags us back into reality, and reminds us that we are no match for death, and there just might be more to this life than what we see and hear each day. Life is more important than accomplishing our greatest temporal dreams. Life is not about how many Facebook likes we have, or how well we maintain our youthful looks. This strange holiday calls into the hereafter. It asks questions about eternity. In this sense, Halloween is like the preacher who prods us, "If you were to die tonight, what would you say to the Judge of the universe?"

Most Christians cannot see this similarity between the preacher's altar call and the Halloween fascination with death, because during Halloween it does not come from the pulpit. Instead it is framed by the creepy images of Zombies and Vampires.

Like the Cowardly Lion, we are afraid of our own shadow, and our own mortality. For this one day each year, we look death in the face and laugh. Halloween challenges our fear of death, and forces us to engage with the issues of our mortality.

Consider how the Bible models the same emphasis of life and death, and sometimes shoves it in our faces:

> *"Now there were some present at that time who told Jesus about the Galileans whose blood Pilate had mixed with their sacrifices. Jesus answered, "Do you think that these Galileans were worse sinners than all the other Galileans because they suffered this way? I tell you, no! But unless you repent, you too will all perish. Or those eighteen who died when the tower in Siloam fell on them—do you think they were more guilty than all the others living in Jerusalem? I tell you, no!*

But unless you repent, you too will all perish." (Luke 13:1-5)

"I looked, and there before me was a pale horse! Its rider was named Death, and Hades was following close behind him. They were given power over a fourth of the earth to kill by sword, famine and plague, and by the wild beasts of the earth." (Revelation 6:8)

"Even though I walk through the darkest valley, I will fear no evil, for you are with me; your rod and your staff, they comfort me." (Psalm 23:4)

"For I am convinced that neither death nor life, neither angels nor demons, neither the present nor the future, nor any powers, neither height nor depth, nor anything else in all creation, will be able to separate us from the love of God that is in Christ Jesus our Lord." (Romans 8:38-39)

"For whoever wants to save their life will lose it, but whoever loses their life for me will find it." (Matthew 16:25)

Halloween and Demon Possession

"The Exorcist", "The Exorcism of Emily Rose", "Poltergiest", and "The Shining": these are part of the repertoire of Halloween. Demonic forces attack humans and attach themselves to the individuals or the things they own. Houses become infected with demonic presences. People become possessed with invisible beings. Priests are called to ward off these evil supernatural forces.

"The Exorcism of Emily Rose" is based upon a true story from Germany. A girl, who was supposedly possessed by a demon, died. The state held trial against the priests who were involved with the possession case to determine if they were negligently responsible for her death. They were found guilty in the actual case. The one priest who played the part for the film was also found guilty in the movie, but the jury asks for the time already served to be the sentence, and in the end of the movie, the audience is left grasping for an explanation of Emily's strange behavior and eventual death. Psychological definitions seem unsatisfactory for the wildness of the situation.

Halloween highlights stories like this. They come to us in both fiction and real life accounts. Salem, Massachusetts has become a central Halloween location in the world, because of this very thing. The Salem Witch Trials of 1692-1693 have been dramatized in popular culture, and studied in history classes across the United States. The idea that demons were blamed in the event is well known, and this is a significant reason that the little city of 42,000 people on the North Shore of Boston is a major tourist destination today. People are drawn to Salem, because of its attachment to the supernatural. The stories of the Puritans who believed they experienced demonic influence are a part of that history.

This section is not meant to be a defense of anybody's doctrine of demon possession, or a description of what occurs in the wildest expressions of psychoses and mental disorders. Nor is this a specific theory of the season of 1692-1693. Theologians, Psychologists, and Historians have written many tomes on these subjects, and you can decide what you think about it after reading their materials. My main point here is that both the popular culture surrounding Halloween and the stories of the Bible are filled with references to this phenomenon. Here a couple examples of stories of demon possession in the Bible:

"They went across the lake to the region of the Gerasenes. When Jesus got out of the boat, a man with an impure spirit came from the tombs to meet him. This man lived in the tombs, and no one could bind him anymore, not even with a chain. For he had often been chained hand and foot, but he tore the chains apart and broke the irons on his feet. No one was strong enough to subdue him. Night and day among the tombs and in the hills he would cry out and cut himself with stones.

When he saw Jesus from a distance, he ran and fell on his knees in front of him. He shouted at the top of his voice, "What do you want with me, Jesus, Son of the Most High God? In God's name don't torture me!" For Jesus had said to him, "Come out of this man, you impure spirit!"

Then Jesus asked him, "What is your name?"

"My name is Legion," he replied, "for we are many." And he begged Jesus again and again not to send them out of the area.

A large herd of pigs was feeding on the nearby hillside. The demons begged Jesus, "Send us among the pigs; allow us to go into them." He gave them permission, and the impure spirits came out and went into the pigs. The herd, about two thousand in number, rushed down the steep bank into the lake and were drowned." (Mark 5:1-13)

"Now the Spirit of the Lord had departed from Saul, and an evil spirit from the Lord tormented him.

Saul's attendants said to him, "See, an evil spirit from God is tormenting you. Let our lord command his servants here to search for someone who can play the lyre. He will play when the evil spirit from God comes on you, and you will feel better."

So Saul said to his attendants, "Find someone who plays well and bring him to me."

One of the servants answered, "I have seen a son of Jesse of Bethlehem who knows how to play the lyre. He is a brave man and a warrior. He speaks well and is a fine-looking man. And the Lord is with him."

Then Saul sent messengers to Jesse and said, "Send me your son David, who is with the sheep." So Jesse took a donkey loaded with bread, a skin of wine and a young goat and sent them with his son David to Saul.

David came to Saul and entered his service. Saul liked him very much, and David became one of his armor-bearers. Then Saul sent word to Jesse, saying, "Allow David to remain in my service, for I am pleased with him."

Whenever the spirit from God came on Saul, David would take up his lyre and play. Then relief would come to Saul; he would feel better, and the evil spirit would leave him." (I Samuel 16:14-23)

Halloween and the Deliverance by Heroes

Soteriology is the study of the doctrines of salvation. Someone should have let the horror movie writers and directors know that what they were doing was soteriological work. Themes of God and the devil, demons and priests, temptation and holiness, dark magic and supernatural protection are balanced in life and death scenarios. Someone ultimately needs salvation from the supernatural dangers, and often there is a savior.

Of course, this is the primary theme in the Bible. Jesus came to save humanity from its sins and errors. Fantasy, sci-fi, comedy, horror literature and their corresponding films play out this soteriological theme over and over. C.S. Lewis' character, Aslan, dies and resurrects. Then he leads the children to a victory over the evil forces that seek to engulf Narnia with its eternal winter. Gandalf appears to die, and returns as the White Wizard. His wisdom and guidance are a primary force in the salvation of Middle Earth. Neo and the Matrix, Superman, Spiderman, and the host of superheroes that fill our comics, movies, and literature are all examples of soteriological themes. Death and destruction are immanent, and someone or something comes to save the day.

Halloween plays this theme over and over with the people who dress themselves in their favorite superhero costumes. Christ is typologically portrayed in each of these costumes. He is our Superman, and he comes to save the day.

Consider how the Bible speaks to this subject, and note how much it feels like the fantastic stories we have grown up with:

> *"...how God anointed Jesus of Nazareth with the Holy Spirit and power, and how he went around doing good and healing all who were under the power of the devil, because God was with him. (Acts 10:38)*
>
> *"Since the children have flesh and blood, he too shared in their humanity so that by his death he might break the power of him who holds the power of death—that is, the devil." (Hebrews 2:14)*

This is a brief outline of some biblical themes of Halloween. A more complete study might include topics such as temptation and sanctification, the balance of free will and predestination, eschatology and the coming of end of the world, angelology and demonology, and the call to be foolish for the sake of the Gospel. For now, it is sufficient to note that Halloween themes are things of the Bible, and give Christianity solid footing to relate to our world in scriptural ways.

Lessons from Halloween in Salem

We live in an age struggling to find definition. We call these times late-modernity, postmodernity, and/or post-Christian. Each of these terms have their respective strengths in helping define the world we live in, but each of the descriptors only capture a small piece in the movement of human social order and the trends of any particular groupthink. Before I get back to Halloween, hold on to your steampunk top hat as I meander through these ideas for a couple pages.

"Postmodern" is the most popular of these terms, but there are scholars and assorted thinkers who believe that what has been called postmodernity, does not exist. For some, the term "late modernity" best defines our times. They say that we remain in the same confines of wild scientific momentum that brought us the progress of modernity. Modernity is typically defined as starting with the Enlightenment and moving to, or through, the Industrial Revolution. We are now living in the unrelenting momentum of the globalization of modern development for those who prefer the term "late-modernity". This is a helpful distinction for understanding the growth of agnosticism, atheism and the worldviews of radical materialists, as well as looking at things like economics and politics.

Yet, another set of thinkers defines our times as postmodern. They describe our world as a post-truth, post-fact, tribal culture. I personally disagree with the manner in which many people interpret the readings of so-called postmodern philosophers like Michel Foucault (who did not use the term about himself), and whose writings I find filled with extremely conservative challenges to increasingly progressive societies. Yet, I prefer the descriptor "postmodern" above other options. If there is any place it seems most applicable, it is in the way American and European societies understand their relationship to religion and spirituality. We live in a culture of pick and choose spirituality. Religious preference often looks more like one's taste in coffee, and less like a search for solid truth. Like going to Starbucks, we have fancy names for variations on themes of a bean, and think that religion is a similar non-critical decision in life. Understanding, that spirituality is viewed by many people today as a self-guided, self-defined category gives us insight into navigating Christian mission in American culture. Strangely, as people are feeling their way through religious experiences, they are simultaneously skeptical about the religious organizational structures, and perhaps this skepticism combined with the continued evolution of one's own spiritual journey best marks the postmodern religious reference point. The old stories about religion are not believed to be valid for today.

A large number of theologians and missionaries believe that we have entered a post-Christian era. We once had basic Christian morals and ethics as a foundation to many aspects of our culture, and stories from the scripture formed a backdrop to our worldviews. It seems that those days are behind us in most places outside the Christian church world.

My years of outreach in Salem have provided lessons about the nature of evangelism in our late-modern/postmodern/post-Christian world, and in this short chapter I will outline some of the principles we have discovered. These are simple lessons that have to do with serving people, befriending people, and maintaining ongoing relationships over the long haul of life. These are also lessons on learning to be uninhibited in our expression of faith, without looking like someone who is out of touch with the world around us.

Find and Need and Fill It

The city of Salem didn't have a decent sound system. The Pizza Fest, the Ice Cream Social, the Halloween Children's Day, and other public events organized by the city all struggled with bad sound, and difficult to hear public announcements. I also noticed that during the Ice Cream Social hundreds of people balanced ice cream bowls in their hands while standing around the park. Along with purchasing a sound system big enough handle full bands and decent sized crowds, we bought an enclosed trailer and turned it into a party wagon. We bought a hundred stackable outdoor chairs for seating, and heavy-duty 10'x10' and 10'x20' canopies to deal with the high likelihood of New England rain. This allowed us to put on our own outdoor events, and to offer and donate our services to the city as well.

This came in most handy on the first Halloween Children's Day we participated in. Suddenly, our tent, and our sound system were center stage for the Children's Day when the city sound system did not arrive. A couple years later, this would prove to be critical. Just barely more than a month after the attack on the Twin Towers on 9-11-2001, we were center stage again during the Salem Halloween Children's Day, and were able to lead hundreds of people from the community through corporate prayers during a difficult time. A few years later, the Haunted Happenings Committee would go through significant changes, and would consider stopping the Children's Day event altogether. Along with the help from Dominic at Domino's Pizza, we saved it from extinction, and would sponsor and run the event for the next 12 years. This all began, because we provided the tents and sound for the Halloween Children's Day on a year when minor disaster might have struck the event. We stepped in to help with our resources.

We found a need and filled it. Sound, tents, and chairs were needed to improve city events, and we invested in those things. Finding a need and filling it is one way we become servants to others, and when we learn to become servants, we learn what it means to be ministers. This was the heart of Jesus, who "made himself of no reputation, and took upon him the form of a servant…." (Philippians 2:7)

Lighten Up and Have Fun

Christians have a tendency to make a big deal about inconsequential things. During Halloween, we are worried about participation in a holiday with unknown origins. Someone using questionable anthropological evidence told us that Halloween was connected to ancient pagan events, and our little church culture bought the story hook, line, and sinker. So as Christians, we keep our kids from going door-to-door with their friends and collecting candy from the generous neighbors. Our friends and acquaintances must think it strange that we are worried about their kids dressing up like Disney princesses and Marvel superheroes for Halloween.

Life with God should be carefree and full of life. This is not to say that we should be careless, and ignorant to the problems of evil, but Halloween in no way looks like the serious problems in our world. It is not sex slavery, or drug addiction. It is not war, cancer, or domestic violence. When we make a big deal about something as innocent as children dressing up for a holiday, we make ourselves irrelevant in our world.

On the other hand, our involvement with events like Halloween displays our ability to express the "fullness of life" we say we've found in Christ. "Fun" is not just a silly word filled with empty activity. The word "fun" has missional implications. Even in the brokenness of this world, Christians can laugh, they can be creative, and they can participate in fun family community events without getting freaked out about minor details or conspiracy theories. Our ability to have fun with the neighbors around us, and still maintain our deep Christian convictions, shows that we know what true joy really is. It shows that we are not making a big deal about little things.

Fun is contagious. It draws people to us. It brings smiles where there once were frowns. It reminds us that most of the difficulties around us are not as over-whelming as we tend to think. Even the most critical difficulties like debilitating disease can be eased with laughter and joy. Fun gives us the opportunity, "to give an answer to everyone who asks you to give the reason for the hope that you have." (1 Peter 3:15)

Too often, we look like Jesus' disciples when they told the children to sit down and be quiet. Jesus rebuked them, and said that the Kingdom was made up of those who were like children. It just might be that a post-Christian world can find hope in a group of strange people who are able to find joy in the simple things of life, are able to express it, and freely lead others into it.

Instead of picketing Halloween, trying to ignore it, or hiding away in our church in serious prayer meetings against the devil, we gave away balloons on Halloween Children's Day, and organized live music on the streets. We offered "Free Psalm Readings", or went door-to-door singing.

Make Your Party the Party to Be At

I looked at Halloween in Salem, and saw a big party. I thought that it might be near impossible for a Christian to get the attention of passing strangers during the massive tourist season. With psychic fairs, museums, haunted houses, vendors selling their wares, and tour businesses giving tours every day throughout the month, getting attention looked impossible. So, my first thought was that we needed to throw a party, and make our party the party people wanted to be at.

Over the years, we organized hug lines and greeted visitors with hugs. We have given away free hot cocoa. We've invited dance schools, and children have danced for their parents. We've invited karate schools, and kids have performed in front of the public. I've seen crowds of thousands cheering for Tenor Brian Landry singing opera on Halloween night, and hundreds of people dancing to the Renegade Sound System or the Mamadou Diop Band, while a group of people dressed as blockheads danced with dinosaurs.

All this fun happens immediately next to our ministry encounter tents. Because people are hanging out at the party, they see opportunities for free spiritual encounters and stand in line, sometimes for over an hour, for "Spiritual Readings" or "Healing Prayers."

The story would sound unbelievable, if I had not watched it for the last nineteen Halloweens. Like the crowds that came out into the wilderness and pressed Jesus for His attention, we have found ourselves over-loaded with ministry opportunity and unable to keep up with it.

Yet, even when we were doing Halloween back in the neighborhoods of Carlsbad, California, we still found a way to make our house the house to visit and hang out at. Games in the garage, and lots of free prizes for kids kept the neighbors around and helped us to develop new relationships in the community.

Love Where You Are and Invest Yourself in It

Salem is unique, and its strangeness is what has driven my passion for involvement in Halloween events. Salem has thirty-one days of Halloween. The economy of the city revolves around tourism, and to a great degree, that tourism revolves around Halloween, Witches, and the history of the Witch Trials.

I could have allowed the strangeness of the small city to fill me with concerns based in late 20th century evangelical urban myths. Instead, I chose to love the place I lived, and looked for a way to invest myself in it.

All it took was a little studious time investment to discover that Halloween was not the demonic holiday 1980 TV Evangelists declared it to be. Their stories did not stand the test of a serious look.

Then it took a little financial investment to participate, and some creative intellectual investment to dream up ideas that were fun for everyone and included sharing God's love.

Investments such as these are investments of service, and have little monetary payback in our world. To do things like this over many years is a sacrifice of service, money, and love. There is a reason churches fall under the corporate structure called "non-profit." It is monetarily unprofitable to us, even while it is profitable to the world.

Wherever you are, love the people, love the place, and invest yourself in whatever ways you can. You may find that this one short season of the year – Halloween, will provide an opportunity to meet new people and create new potentials for the Gospel.

Treat Every Place Like a Mission Field

You should walk out your front door like you are traveling to a far away place to become a missionary to a new culture. People who have been raised in evangelical Christianity are part of a subculture in their own countries. Often, we do not understand the world around us. That world is contrary to the things we know about God, and to true religion. It is as though the dominant culture, and the popular subcultures around us speak other languages.

If we were to approach the cultures around us like a missionary prepares for the mission field, we would study them. We would find out why people do what they do, how they gather, and what traditions and daily rituals are important to them. After a season of study, we would hunt for things in culture that naturally incline people to the Gospel.

This principle of living like missionaries in our own culture naturally leads to one of the most important lessons I have learned:

Find Shadows of the Gospel in Culture

My chapter on the biblical values of Halloween highlights this practice. It is the task of the mission minded Christian to find ways to communicate biblical truths already built into the cultures around us. Every culture, and every subculture has hints of God's truth built into it. Goth subculture often focuses on the death and darkness elements found in the Bible with more honesty than most churches do. Neo-Pagans are interested in the supernatural, and exhibit a more concentrated discipline toward supernatural practices than most Pentecostals. They take it seriously and feel a responsibility to spiritual things. Their practices may not be the kind of spirituality found in Christianity, but their discipline sometimes puts us to shame.

Too often, evangelical Christians feel the need limit the Gospel to only a few truths: You are a sinner, Jesus died for your sins, if you believe in Him you will go to heaven, and if you don't you will go to hell. Limiting our communication of biblical truth to these things also limits our communication about many truths in a world in need of truth discovery.

Truths about hope, the miraculous, responsibility to the poor, caring for the earth, moral integrity, and honesty are all part of a message God is bringing to people on earth. Truths related to sin and temptation, heaven and hell, angels and demons, God and Satan, death and salvation are already part of the Halloween motif. This should make adjustment to the holiday an easy thing for the Christian. Halloween is better positioned than almost any other season of the year to focus on the issues of life and death, and it refuses to allow us to ignore the implications of death.

All these elements create scenarios for Gospel communication, but because Halloween is a joyous celebration, it requires that we find creative and fun ways to focus on these issues. This is one of the most important things to learn from Halloween. If we can communicate these wild Gospel truths to people during Halloween, and capture their interest, we can learn to do it every day of the year, no matter how hardened people appear to be against Christianity.

For a number of years, our church met on the walking mall on Essex Street in Salem. Essex Street is the place most of Salem's million visitors will pass, and so, they all passed our front doors. We met in an old bank building, and when you looked through the front doors, you saw a massive double door vault at the end of the room. We left the front doors open during the Halloween season, and invited people to spend time with us. Dream Interpreters modeling their practice after Daniel sat in small groups around the room, people were available to pray for you, and others had a deck of cards called the Jesus Deck that was filled with stories from the four suits of the cards: Matthew Mark, Luke and John.

All our practices during the Halloween season were designed to find the shadows of Gospel truth in the Halloween season and use them to share God's love.

Don't Avoid Hard Biblical Truths

In the chapter about visiting Salem, I told the story of my friend Rick MacDonald playing the part of Jonathan Edwards as I played a carnival barker and set the stage for his message: "Sinners in the Hands of an Angry God." People enjoyed the interactive element of shouting, "Amen" and "Save us!" Meanwhile, street preachers passed out Gospel tracts and received a response fit for traitors. Those who were being mocked by the crowd comforted themselves with the belief that the abuse they suffered was a natural occurring persecution due to the hardness of the hearts of the Halloween celebrants. Yet, they spoke about the love of God and were rejected, and we spoke about Hell and Judgment, and people appreciated the historical reenactment of Jonathan Edward's "Sinners in the Hands of an Angry God." The street preachers had few interactions that evening, and many of those interactions were confrontational. We on the other hand spent the entire evening talking to dozens of people and making friends while discussing (not preaching about) things like Hell, Judgment, and forgiveness.

During our engagement with people celebrating Halloween, we discovered that creative and fun illustrations about the ideas related to difficult subjects was easy and natural, but we also discovered that it was not the subject matter itself, but the presentation of the subject that mattered.

On the one hand, we spend lots of time blessing people and letting them know how much God loves them, yet, we were not afraid to visit the subjects already inherent to the horror aspects of Halloween.

Don't Be Afraid to Be Jesus to People in Secular Celebrations

It's easy for us to imagine Jesus hanging out with sinners and sharing His life and love with them. Why then, can't we see ourselves in the same scenarios? Why are we afraid to do what He did? And, why do we feel like it is a compromise to our faith to behave like Jesus behaved during the time He walked the earth?

It is our task to be "God with skin on" to the world around us. Whoever first penned, or spoke those words, found a perfect quip to create a wise missional sound bite.

Being God with skin on does not necessitate carrying protest signs declaring our dislike, or God's supposed dislike, of this world. We do not need bullhorns or soapboxes. We do not need to navigate every conversation to a conclusion of telling someone that "Jesus died for you." In fact, sometimes we can just smile, or offer a helping hand. We could give an encouraging word, or create a work of art. We can organize a game night, or give away Snickers candy bars because, "God has created a funny old world that makes me snicker."

The words, "Preach the Gospel at all times, and if necessary use words", have been attributed to Saint Francis. It is unlikely he ever said this. In fact, if there is any place this concept finds its home it is with the Desert Fathers and Mothers. In the 2nd through 6th century, hordes of people fled the oppression of the Roman Empire with the troubles of war, poverty, and corruption and left their homes behind. With a newfound faith they sought solitude and the freedom to practice their new religion in the wildernesses of Egypt, Syria, and eventually as far abroad as Wales and Ireland. To the Desert Fathers and Mothers, living the scripture was of greater value than speaking the scriptures. They believed that if someone could not live the words of scripture, they were not worthy to declare those words to others.

Although, I believe it is critical to share our faith in words, it is even more critical to live them, and this is particularly true at this point in history, when distrust in Organized Religion may be at an all time high. Being in the public eye, and living our public lives with integrity is a critical witness to our world.

When the World Visits, Become a Gatekeeper

Salem has only 42,000 people living in it, but it might be the most famous city of 42,000 in the world. When I tell people around the globe that I live in Salem, they immediately respond with questions about "witches", and typically make an interesting crinkled-up face.

I recently spent a week in the tiny village of Avebury, England. A good part of the village sits inside the more famous ancient stone circle by the same name, and the surrounding area is known as one of the hot spots for crop circles in the UK. Consequently, over a million tourists will visit Avebury throughout the year. I spoke at a small weekend gathering at the Anglican Church, and encouraged the people to view their small parish as a greeting place to the world. I was surprised to see how encouraged they were by these words. Not all people who have a heart for missions have the ability to travel to far away places, but many of us live in places where the world is coming to us – even little places like Salem, Massachusetts; Penzance, Cornwall; Avebury and Glastonbury, England; and Caernarfon, Wales. Every tourist destination, and festival location is a place that punches above its weight. Their influence in this world is disproportionate to their size, and for this reason, Christians should be active in these places, and should find ways to be a positive influence to visitors.

I have heard churches describe themselves as "gatekeepers" for their cities and their regions without actually spending any time with the visitors and travelers who pass through their towns. We are not "gatekeeping" if we are not active when and where the people come and go.

Stories from Nineteen Years of Halloween

Here are some of the many stories from the experiences of the thousands of people who have joined us during our nineteen years of outreach in Salem. Some of these stories are mine. Others include people from Salem and nearby cities and towns, people from all across the United States, and others from Great Britain. They are Baptists, Anglicans, Pentecostals, and people from a variety of Christian traditions. Many of the stories are life changing experiences for the person ministering, in other cases the people who receive ministry have experienced something life changing.

Some of these stories are simple non-dramatic events describing personal transformation. Others are miraculous stories describing God's intervention in someone's life. There are stories involving the presentation of social justice issues, and stories of relationship building with people who are typically believed to be antagonistic to Christianity.

One of the things we seldom share is the number of who ask to pray with us to become Christians. First of all, we do not think the people we minister to should ever be treated like numbers, and second, I am not convinced that a formal Sinner's Prayer is solid evidence that someone has entered into a real relationship with God. Nonetheless, consistently over the last nineteen years, each year somewhere between thirty and forty people ask to pray with the people ministering on the streets with us for God's forgiveness and strength to walk with Him daily. These are typically unsolicited requests, because we avoid, at all costs, sounding like we are selling Jesus.

Many of our stories include our Pagan friends Our stories in Salem will not sound like Halloween ministry stories anywhere else, because there is no place with such a high concentration of Witchcraft and Neo-Paganism as Salem.

The stories come from so many different Christian denominations and non-denominational groups, that some of them might appear strange to you, while others will be exciting. What I hope you gain from this set of testimonies is the heart of the people learning to minister in a setting as alternative as Halloween in Salem, Massachusetts.

This first story illustrates an assumption I have about God: that God is already working in people's lives long before we meet them. In this case, God had prepared a young man by using his dreams, and I was there to interpret his night vision.

When God Visits in Dreams

One evening close to Halloween, a young man in an elegant, long black ceremonial cape stood in line with his friends. I had trained a few people to interpret dreams that year. I was taking a break from working inside the tent, and I was keeping the line outside happy. The caped man and I chatted. He discovered I was a pastor, and we discussed the differences between his Pagan path, and my Christian worldview in a friendly manner. For the most part I asked questions, and he answered them. He believed the spiritual realm was a helpful, friendly place. If he asked for guidance and help, the spirits would not lead him astray, and I shared my position, believing that there are deceiving spirits just as there are deceiving people on earth.

After talking for some time, he asked about dream interpretation, and wondered if I interpreted dreams. I told him I did. He told me his dream:

He and his friends were visiting Red Rock, Colorado. It is a New Age "hot spot", a natural amphitheater, and beautiful concert venue. After some time of looking around Red Rock, black helicopters came racing over the hills, and began to shoot at him and his friends. Some of his friends died. Others were severely wounded. He and one other friend were able to escape into nearby caves, and hide from the helicopters. Then the dream ended.

"What do you think this means?" he asked.

I looked at him, and paused for dramatic effect. Then I said, "The spiritual realm is not always benign, sometimes it is malignant and harmful."

The young man gasped out loud. His eyes opened wide, and he said, "You are so right!"

I had not thrown Bible verses at him to argue from a biblical standpoint that demons existed, and spiritual deception was real. This was a young man who had studied religions, and understood many of the basics of Christianity. He had rejected the Christianity he was familiar with, and adopted another religious view, but his rejection of the Bible did not mean that he rejected all spiritual voices. He took stock in his own dreams, and that evening his dreams and my Christian worldview met.

When he would not listen to the Bible, he would listen to his dreams. I believe the God Who wrote the words of scripture had visited his dreams by night.

This next story is a unique example of developing positive relationships with the Neo-Pagan community. Each year, a handful of bull-horn toting street preachers come into town, and typically cause a bit of trouble by stirring up the local population with their hell fire and brimstone preaching. From time to time the preachers will harass the local Neo-Pagans and Witches by standing in front of the Witchcraft Shops and troubling their customers. Sometimes, the police are called to intervene, but on one occasion, it was our group of costumed monks, who wandered around the city blessing people, that responded to the call for help.

The Day the Monks Saved the Witches from the Street Preachers:

About 10 years ago, I received a call on a weekend just before Halloween. A friend of mine, a male Witch, who runs a large psychic fair was in a panic.

"Pastor Phil, help! The street preachers are harassing our workers and our customers. I don't know what to do."

I turned to the young men who were taking a lunch break from walking around Salem dressed as monks blessing people and said, "The Psychic Fair is asking for help. The Street Preachers are harassing them." So James, looked at the others guys, and said, "Dude! Let's monk up!"

So, they monked up. They put their robes back on, and went down the street to the Psychic Fair, and they arrived to pandemonium.

The preachers were preaching and the Witches were screaming.

"Witchcraft is an abomination to God!"

"What gives you the right to do this?"

One Street Preacher was trying to cast a demon out of one of the Witches. "Come out you foul beast!"

"Get away from me!"

A crowd was watching all this as placards were waving, and Witches were crying. One Witch threatened to call the police and press assault charges, because a Street Preacher got a little pushy.

The Monks stood between the Witches and the Street Preachers, and began to talk to the Preachers about acting in love. Of course, the Preachers didn't take too kindly to messing up their mission. They accused the Monks of being in league with the devil, but about 45 minutes later, the Street Preachers were disbanding, and the Witches were profusely thanking the Monks for defusing the situation.

If you visit Salem on some Halloween, and go to the Psychic Fair, or visit the Dream Interpretation booth, you might hear the story about the day the Monks saved the Witches from the Street Preachers.

The following story comes from a prayer meeting during the Halloween season in 2012:

Witches Dancing in My Church

It was shortly before midnight leading up to Halloween morning. Our little church in Salem, MA was holding all night prayer gatherings, and this was the last of 3 consecutive 12am to 6am prayer and worship meetings.

Only a few people gathered each night, because most of us were working day and night in outreach activities, and had been doing so every weekend for the entire month. Now there was only one day of ministry to go. It was the last push, and the tens of thousands of visitors coming to our little city on Halloween Night would be arriving in about 12 hours.

Our church has some interesting friends, and they heard about the worship and prayer gathering. They wanted to join us, and of course, we figured that anyone who wants to join a prayer meeting ought to be encouraged to do so.

April, who had organized and was leading the prayer gathering was still involved in ministry outreach when midnight struck, so I plugged in my guitar, and sat at the microphone. I sang a song in Welsh, which I had written just a few months earlier: "Mae dy gariad 'yn nghario fi" (Your Love Carries Me).

As I sang, some of the people who were staying for the meeting began to gather. There were eight or nine of us who were either part of the church, or friends who had traveled from distant places to be part of this October outreach. Then, there were two visiting Witches. They had come to Salem from New Jersey, one was the "Queen Mother," and the other was studying under her leadership. Then there was also a group of Gnostic friends of ours - not "Gnostic" in the general sense of the word as it is used by pastors and armchair theologians, but "Gnostic" as a description they chose for their own spirituality.

Soon, Christopher (my Christian friend from Texas) was dancing to my song, and others were singing the chorus along with me in both Welsh and

English. I finished singing and April took the mic at the piano. She led some prayers, played a song, and then the group morphed into becoming a drum circle.

Soon the Witches and the Gnostics joined the drum circle in a joyous, raucous noise. I sang out, "Feel the wind of the Spirit, Taste the goodness of the Spirit, Let the power of the Spirit fall on us!" and "Jesus my King is coming with grace, coming with love, coming with power," and a few other straight up Pentecostal sounding spontaneous prayer songs.

Sometime during that drum circle, three young men who had joined us earlier in the day for outreach ministry came to the prayer meeting. They were part of a YWAM (Youth With A Mission) team visiting Salem for the weekend.

They stood in the back, and watched the peculiar gathering. During that time, the "Queen Mother" took the lead drum, and led the rhythm, and as one might expect from an elegant African American Witch – she had rhythm. A friend of mine who probably most closely identifies as a Gnostic was playing his wooden flutes to the drumming. The drumming, singing, and dancing went on, and on, and on. The YWAM youth stayed for about 40 minutes, looking like deer caught in the headlights. As the drum circle slowed to a stop they left the meeting.

Now I was quite surprised that everyone seemed quite comfortable. Although only myself and April had lead in prayers and songs in that first hour, no one was bothered by the clear Christian implications of our prayers. In fact, everyone had a great time.

Well, except maybe the YWAM boys, or so it seemed.

A little after 1am, a few of us headed home to get some sleep before the Halloween Day outreach activities were to begin. Along the way, we ran into the guys from YWAM, who were still up, and wandering around the city.

"Now, wasn't that the whackiest prayer meeting you've ever seen – with Witches, and Gnostics and all?" I asked.

One of the guys responded, "I tried really hard to be offended, but I couldn't. There was too much love in the room."

I'm not sure that revival looks like Witches dancing in my church on Halloween, but it sure felt like it was darn close to it, and strangely enough, these are not just my Christian friends. We are from wildly different worldviews, and are probably causing equal amounts of trouble in our respective worlds.

Some of our outreach events are based upon a carnivalesque approach to ministry. People expect one thing, but we want to surprise them and turn their world upside down. This next story is one of the most dramatic experiences we've seen in the nineteen years of outreach.

One Big Sorry Church

It was no new idea. We read about it in Donald Miller's book Blue Like Jazz. James had the idea of trying it in Salem over the weekends of Halloween events, and I thought it would work well, but we had no idea how well.

James bought a few monks robes. We had the tents and tables. James and Brooke brought some candles and incense. We made signs, "Free Confessional Booth."

At first people walked by and laughed. Occasionally someone would say nervously, "I don't have the time. It would take all day."

Then a few people began to trickle into the tent, and sit for a confession. They would walk out with big eyes, and occasionally some tears. Things began to gain some momentum when some of my friends who run a Psychic Faire decided to give it a try.

"What do you do in there?"

"Confessions." Jeff said frankly with a twist of wry. Jeff does wry well.

"But what happens in there?"

"I can't tell you. You will have to experience it for yourself." Jeff said, and after a pause, "But it's not what you expect."

"What do you mean?"

"I can't tell you. Are you up for giving it a try?" Jeff asked with that wry smirk sneaking out from the corner of his mouth again.

They entered the tent as a group. The three sat together in support of one another. Witches entering a Christian confessional booth need backup. Who knows what gallows, or stake piled high with dry faggots hides behind the tent?

James spoke first, "Thank you for joining us in the confession booth. I'm sure you nervously entered expecting to share your deepest, darkest secrets, but here we are offering another kind of confession. We want to confess on behalf of the church."

This was the beginning of a deeply moving time for my friends, the Witches. I found them half and hour later standing in front of the confessional booth with tears still streaming down their faces.

"This is the most moving spiritual experience I've ever had," she said dragging long on her cigarette.

"I have been waiting for so many years to hear something like this. This is the high point of my Samhain." His makeup was running as he continued to cry.

James and the other monks confessed the sins of the church over the ages to my Witch friends. He apologized for the Burning Times, the Inquisitions, and the Witch Trials in Salem. He apologized for the Crusades. He apologized for the prejudice and fear in the church that has caused people to respond to Witches with anger and personal attacks. James confessed for being part of a church, which imposed its morality upon the Witches, even though they had made no decision to follow Jesus.

Later that day other Witches began to come through the tent. An entire Psychic Fair of Readers and Seers came through the tent. Witches from shops around town heard the rumors circulating about the confessional booth, and came to visit. They all came with the expectation of confessing their sins, and left with a heart warming twist. That year nearly forty Neo-Pagans visited our confessional booth. The tears were many, and the hearts of people generally antagonistic to Christianity were endeared to us.

Toward the end of the day, a Tarot Reader brought one of her clients into the tent because, "she needed to hear this."

We are one big sorry church, and that has been our strength.

We've had a number of stories about people who have been prayed for and the healing that they have experienced. This story is the most dramatic we have heard. Initially, Denise contacted the city asking who ran the healing tent. The city contacted me, and I put her in touch with Tim Arroyo and Jamie Dickson from the Love Project who organized the tent. This is her story below.

Miracles on the Street

In April of 2017 I was diagnosed with stage four metastatic breast cancer. My oncologist said I could expect to live for maybe four or five more years. The doctors made a plan for an eighteen-week chemo regimen to be followed by surgery to remove tumors from my breast, liver and lymph nodes followed by radiation treatments. The tumors were each over six centimeters and there was also cancer in some of my lymph nodes.

I underwent six very aggressive chemo treatments from May through August. It made me very sick and weak. In late September I started feeling a little better and thought that before I had to have the surgery that it would be really nice to go on a short vacation with my family. I was afraid that in the short time I had left that I may not find the strength to ever do that again.

We live in Erie, Pennsylvania but for about a year when my daughter was very young we lived in Lewiston, Maine. It's always beautiful in New England in the fall so I thought it would be nice to take my daughter back there to see our old home because she really had no memory of it.

We made our trip to New England the weekend before Halloween. We spent some of our time in Salem, Massachusetts during their Halloween festivities. The weather was gorgeous and there were thousands of people all over the town.

As we made our way through the crowded streets I noticed a tent with signs that read, "Free Healing." I was intrigued, especially because of my current health issues. I approached the tent and came upon a young man who gave me a very friendly smile. I said, "Hello" to him and told him I was interested in what they were doing. He asked me what was going on in my life and I told him about my cancer diagnosis.

He took me by the hand and asked me if I wanted to go inside the tent and pray with some of their members. I agreed and we went inside. He introduced me to three young people named Leah, Rachel and Michael. I explained my situation to them. They were very sympathetic and caring.

We prayed together for a while and Rachel put her hands on my abdomen. She asked Jesus to take the cancer away. We prayed some more and then we just sat and talked quietly for a while. I got very emotional while we talked. I wanted so badly for our prayers to be answered. Realistically though it just seemed like more than I could hope for.

Before I got up to leave Leah asked me if I felt anything when Rachel laid her hands on me. She said some others had told them that they had felt a warm sensation or tingling. I had not experienced anything like that but I told them that what I did feel was like a huge weight had been lifted off of my shoulders.

A week or so after I returned home from New England I went to see all of my doctors. They were all amazed. The results of my most recent PET Scan showed no evidence of disease. My cancer had gone into remission.

They couldn't explain it. The four of them all told me the only explanation was that I had received a miracle.

I did not have to have any of the surgery that they had planned and I did not have to have any radiation treatments. My tumors have continued to shrink and only the one in my liver is still visible on the scans. It is now only about seven millimeters in size.

I had always been a faithful Christian and had strong religious beliefs. I had been praying so hard for months for a miracle. Many of my friends and family members had been praying for that too. Imagine my surprise when I received it.

The power of prayer is real. I truly believe that I was called to Salem that weekend. I believe that God brought me there to meet the members of the Love Project so that they could deliver the power of his healing to me.

I will be forever grateful to God and for the miracle I have received thanks in great part to those young people who prayed with me that day.

- *Denise Edmonds Fulton, Girard, PA*

Frequently, events during Halloween will surprise us, and one of the most surprising things is to have Neo-Pagans ask for our help or our advice. This has become a common theme for us during the Halloween season in Salem.

When Witches Ask for Help

In the ninth October of ministry in Salem's month long Haunted Happenings events, we now had over a hundred volunteers. The members of our own small church, interns from a prophetic school of ministry, groups from other churches in the area, musicians, and people who travelled from as far away as California joined us to "do the stuff."

I taught classes on understanding Neo-Paganism to people who visited to do evangelism in our unique gentle style. We held events specifically aimed at offering fun, yet significant experiences to visiting tourists. We served free hot cocoa on the streets, and provided seven days of live music on the city's longest running outdoor stage, which we paid for, sponsored, and ran.

During this unbelievably busy season a man from New York joined us, and stayed at our house for a week. We prayed together. We practiced the ancient art of scripture meditation called Lectio Divina. We wandered around town and visited some of the Witches I knew, and I taught him what I had learned over the last 13 years of befriending Witches.

The man from New York had come with in hopes of discovering a new way to do evangelism, after having felt ineffective over most of the course of his twenty-three years as a Christian. The year before he heard about our outreach in Salem, and his heart had been stirred to visit us. One afternoon he and I were doing Dream Interpretation (pretending to be like Daniel of the Bible) at the church. As we were interpreting dreams, an acquaintance arrived in his long black cape and some convincing looking vampire fangs. He patiently waited for us to conclude our session. Vlad was a Goth magician working in the city. He had visited our church once before, and he and I frequently spoke on the street. When we completed our session, Vlad asked if I could visit one of the local Witches, who had become quite frustrated, and was apparently in some state of frenzy that day.

"Pastor Phil, he respects you, and I am sure he will listen to you." Vlad said.

When we were free, we made our way to try and help this professional Witch who was working his way toward burnout. I mentioned that this had now become a fairly regular request, especially during the busy Halloween season.

Unfortunately, we could not reach this Witch in his shop on our little journey down the street. So we let it be known we were making a friendly call, and went on our way. As we left the store we met another local Pagan shop owner. He asked me if I would help bring peace between feuding business owners.

"Could you do a miracle?" He asked.

"Sure, what's going on?"

He told of two business owners: one who ran a haunted house, and another who ran a Witch shop. They were at odds with one another over what he thought was fairly petty issues.

"It would be better for business for all of us if they could get along," he said.

I told him I would give it a try, and as we walked away the man from New York laughed with wonder and said, "Two different Pagans have asked for your help and counsel for their friends in the last twenty minutes. This is incredible!"

Some of our ministry tactics border on the edges of craziness, but then so does Halloween. The crazier the experience, the more it fits into the Halloween ethos. This next story comes from one of these crazier moments.

The Witch and the Bank Vault

She screamed from inside the locked vault.

I closed only one of the two massive doors of our double-doored vault. As I turned the handle, the gentle clicking noise accompanied the narrowing of the thin crack of light until it disappeared altogether. Then she screamed all the louder, but these were faint and distant cries to us.

Within the locked vault a person cannot see their hand in front of their face. Utter darkness envelopes you, and no amount of time will allow your eyes to adjust to see even faint images.

I allowed her to scream a short time - short for me, but perhaps an eternity for her. After about 45 seconds I spun the handle counter-clockwise, and the gentle clicking gave way to the fine crack of light, and then to the opening of the door.

She was free again. The Witch who was a mother of two young children emerged from the Vault. She was cursing, and shouting, and confessing sins, and saying she did not deserve this.

We listened. We laughed. We discussed the experience with her.

She described the complete feeling of isolation, and the sense of truly understanding the concept of Hell as outer darkness.

She said thank you – repeatedly.

After she left, I scratched my head, and considered this strange, but remarkable interaction.

She had come into our church meeting space. It was a 200-year-old bank, with a massive vault at the end of the room. She came with her friend. Both were dressed mildly witchy in black, with tall shoes.

We discussed our upcoming event called "The Brimstone Chronicles." "The Brimstone Chronicles" walked through the history of Christian concepts of death, and the afterlife. It included a full feast and among other things, an experience in "outer darkness". People would be asked to consider outer darkness, as they were locked in the old vault for a short time.

She was excited about the concept, and asked to be locked in the vault. We asked if she was sure she wanted to do this. She was insistent, and stated that we should not open the door even if we heard her screaming. We obliged, and the strange story of screaming, cursing, confessing sins, and thanking us for the experience unfolded.

A couple weeks later she returned on a Sunday afternoon. She was walking through downtown Salem with her mother.

"Mom, this is Pastor Phil," she smiled proudly, "Pastor Phil, this is my mother."

"I've heard so much about you. It is nice to be able to put a face to the name." Her mother replied.

We spoke awhile, and even reminisced about the experience with outer darkness. My friend the Witch had asked for Hell. We gave it to her, and we were still friends. Her Roman Catholic mother thanked me for being a positive influence. They left.

I scratched my head again.

Testimonies from Those Who Have Joined Us

For me, the Haunted Happenings outreach was a first for many things. I quickly realized that in addition to never traveling to Salem before, it was a bit intimidating attending my first formal outreach and giving my first prophetic words in an environment swarming with psychics and witches. Once we began to minister, however, I saw how the thirst of the people in Salem for deep spirituality drew the presence of the Holy Spirit in such a thick and powerful way. I no longer needed to worry about performing because it was not me touching those people anyway.

– Kyle

My experience at Haunted Happenings in Salem, Massachusetts was a life changing one. I've never felt so much overwhelming love in my heart for complete strangers before. I went into this outreach doubting the Lord's ability to move and left with a much greater knowledge of His unconditional love for His people.

– Jourdan

What I personally took away from the day was a deep sense of the Father's urgent yet patient love for His lost sheep and the exhilaration of being able to participate in the revelation of that love to them. Giving prophetic words puts us in a place where we are given a glimpse of God's perspective and it forever changes our vision.

– Olivia

A young woman came to our team looking to have a re-occurring dream interpreted. She had dreamed several times over the last ten years about snakes in her bed. It would terrify her so much she would jump out of bed screaming. She admitted that she is generally terrified of snakes even in the natural. We felt the meaning of the dream was simply that her general fear was so great it was ruining her rest. Upon sharing this with her, she began to open up to us about her fears. She seemed to have a great deal of trust in us even before sharing the dream but as we talked further her trust grew. After talking through some of the sources of her fear, she explained to us that she has recently left the Mormon Church of which her family is still heavily involved and even has family ancestry that can be traced to Joseph Smith, the father of Mormonism. Upon her sharing this, a marvelous shift came in the atmosphere. Though her experience was marked with harassment for leaving Mormonism both from the people in her life and from the spiritual realm, we suddenly saw in her a courageous and bold seeker of Truth. And in that moment we watched as her concept of God transformed before our eyes. He went from being a dictator that cruelly demanded things of her to a great big Goodness that Loved her immensely and knew her intimately! The Presence of God became so heavy and sweet as we communicated this to her that all of us were moved to tears. I found myself filled with awe as God revealed to all of us (including this precious woman) what He felt about her. It was truly an honor to meet this over comer and to encourage her that, contrary to what others may have pressed on her, she is on the right path as God draws her into her destiny!

–Ali Carter

I was standing outside of our ministry tents with a group of us that were doing "healings" and "spiritual encounters." A lady came out from being ministered to and said, "It was okay, but I wish they had said something about my eyes." I overheard her say that and then I asked her, "What's wrong with your eyes?" She then began to say, "No, it's ok I am not going to worry about it." Again I said, "No seriously what's wrong with your eyes I really want to know?" She began to tell me how she has Macular Degeneration and is losing her eyesight. I told her that my Grandfather has the same disease and was one of the first people to receive all the experimental tests. This instantly gave me favor. I then asked if I could pray for her. As I prayed she took off her glasses and began to look around. At first she said it was a little better but the second time I prayed she yelled, "Oh my God I can read that guys shirt!" While praying, I watched as the cloudiness in her eyes began to shrink to just a small spot in the corner of her left eye. As we prayed one last time she cried, gave me a big hug and then disappeared into the crowd.

– Brandon Crummer

For the first time, this year a number of our friends and family invested in our efforts. Dozens of our friends partnered with us to raise $800 so that we could match equal exchange's gift and make our hot cocoa slave free. That was excellent (and expect the ask will be repeated next year so that we can take our cups down the bio-degradable route)! My own family and close friends donated $1100 in operating support to our little adventure. Those dollars came in quite handy during a year when The Gathering has found it difficult to keep our heads above water, much less purchase supplies for the outreach. We were seriously humbled by the generosity of our friends and family. Thank you for honoring God by setting us free to serve!

On Hallows Eve and Halloween the incomparable Anita and her "not for sale" crew offered people an opportunity to experience "death by chocolate" for a second year. This was the second year to host this event, we had over 300 guests attend and many, many more folks than last year were interested in discussing fair trade and acting upon what they had learned.

Did I mention how amazing Carrie was throughout the whole Halloween season? I had no idea how she would take to it, but within minutes of starting she was barking at guests in the street, anchoring the cocoa booth, dancing with strangers dressed as gasoline. Seriously, she was amazing.

– Jeff Gentry

After outlining the generosity of people who helped support our Free Hot Cocoa service and helped us serve Fair Trade Hot Cocoa, Jeff highlights the work of people dressing as monks and blessing people on the streets:

Jessie and Libby and the good folks from their home church in Beverly "monked up" on Halloween and spent six hours in the street laying hands on and blessing people they had never met. I didn't have the courage to do anything more than serve hot cocoa during my first experience in 2003, so I was amazed by their boldness!

Ben, the Independent Baptist from Maine carved an unexpected niche by becoming the master of the Jesus Deck and a spot on dream interpreter as well. I wasn't sure how much time he could commit, but he consistently under-promised and over-delivered and we were all so blessed by his presence.

– Jeff Gentry

The following story comes from the Prof. Carlos Zeisel, one of the crew from The Gathering. Carlos worked interpreting dreams, and doing what we call Spiritual Readings. Here is what Carlos had to say about his experiences:

I was on a team with Drew and Beth from the Bridge Church and we were doing Spiritual Readings for about an hour. A woman came who said that she had a dream. The dream was an invitation from God to join him on his earthly kingdom. I did not realize that she connected with me, and Drew said "Carlos why don't you begin and help this woman invite Christ into her heart." She had already agreed to accept Christ because of the revelation from the dream and the spiritual readings. You must understand I had never said the sinner's prayer or accepted Christ in the typical way, so I felt awkward in trying to do it with this woman. But I went forward like a child trying to not look stupid in front of a class. I was blown away and she thanked us. A week later she returned and thanked me again. I was in awe how the Holy Spirit helped move this woman into a relationship with Christ.

– Prof. Carlos Zeisel

The Dos and Don'ts of Halloween

Don't get freaked out by the gory aspects of Halloween.

Yes, some people go overboard, but then again so did Grimm's Fairy Tales, and so did some of the descriptions of war, sickness, depravity and suicide in the Bible. There is a strong connection between death and apocalyptic scenarios in literature and film, and these connections carry spiritual meaning. From stories of zombies, vampires, monsters, and antichrists we find interesting correlations to finding safety in God during apocalyptic crises, and social commentary and critique is ripe even in story lines like The Walking Dead.

Take advantage of the community openness.

What other day of the year will people happily open their doors to a knock from a weirdly dressed stranger saying funny things to them? In fact, they will be so happy to see you that they will give you a gift. How often does that happen? You couldn't get that to happen on Christmas Day while everyone is excitedly opening packages under the decorated piney tree.

Don't get all caught up in the supposed dark intentions of the night.

How many Witches do you actually know? My guess is that most people reading this will answer "none." I know hundreds – literally hundreds. That is because I live in Salem Massachusetts, and have friends in the Neo-Pagan and Witchcraft community from around the world. I have yet to encounter any dead kitty cats, or sacrificed babies. I have found very few examples of curses upon churches or individual Christians. I am not saying that there are not any examples of curses by Witches, but the Witches I know are generally kind people who want the world to be a better, more peaceful place. For this reason, I do not have to hide on Halloween to pray the darkness away. The Witches I know can be treated as regular people, and Halloween can be treated as any other day with people gathering together in large numbers.

Join someone doing something both fun and redemptive, if you can.

Because I am in Salem, and 500,000 to a million people will visit our city in October, we provide live music on the streets, give away free hot cocoa, free hugs, and will set up booths to offer a variety of spiritual counseling services. This is our way of connecting to a searching world during a searching season.

Some Simple Ideas for Getting Started

As you consider beginning to get involved with outreach during Halloween, remember, that even outside Salem, Massachusetts, Halloween is usually longer than one day. You should think of Halloween as a season. People all across the US and now in other nations are celebrating the day, and preparing for it long before it arrives. At least consider Halloween Day, and the weekend before as part of the same celebration.

I am not going to pretend to know what specific skill sets you or the people in your church have. I do not know your neighborhood, or how the people in your city or town celebrate the Halloween season.

Unfortunately, most Halloween church ideas are viewed as alternatives to Halloween. They are not truly Halloween participation events. The result is that we have looked like protestors in a community celebration, and our protests appear petty.

Some years ago, a young man came to Salem on Halloween. He wore a pair of nicely pressed dark brown slacks, and white button up shirt, buttoned to the top, and a thin black tie. He had pens tucked neatly in his shirt pocket, and he walked around Salem in his black dress shoes carrying a tall protest sign that said, "You Are All Going to Hell." Periodically, the crowd would begin booing, and when the booing reached a fevered pitch, the young man would pull a string, and his sign would roll up to reveal the words, "Just Kidding! Happy Halloween!" and the people would cheer. When Christians get involved with Halloween in fun and redemptive ways, it causes a similar response. People are relieved and get excited that we are out there.

I am only going to give a handful of ideas, because this book has already been peppered with stories of our Halloween activities through the years. So assuming that you have an interest in participating in reaching out to people on one of the most open and interesting times of the year, here just a few starting ideas:

- Has your church got a good choir? Why don't you send them out door-to-door singing Gospel songs, and giving gifts to the neighbors?
- Do you have a Garage, a yard, or a room in the house that can be converted into a game room for the neighborhood trick-or-treaters? Perhaps even your church can

become a place for children's events on Halloween.

- Consider setting up a Spiritual Advice Booth, or a Healing Prayer Booth if your town has Halloween celebrations.
- Dress up in costumes with a message, and be as wild and creative as possible. When we wandered around town as monks offering "Free Blessings," we were amazed at how many people stopped us and asked for a free blessing.
- Find as many ways to be generous as possible. Give in a way that makes the children and the parents want to return to your house every year.

Burning Religion:

navigating the impossible space between religion and secular society

This is the first part of something Phil hopes will become his Magnum Opus. It is a wild combination of philosophy, history, psychology, theology and fantasy tales patterned after medieval literature such as Dante, Cervantes and Rabelais.

Burning Religion sets the struggle between religion and secular society in a context that makes the struggle a model for all the categories that divide us. The revolutionary solution to navigating our differences is found in a most unconventional place.

Witches Are Real People Too:

understanding American Neo-Paganism from a Christian perspective

In the summer of 1997, two Pentecostal Christian ministers opened a locked gate on a remote dirt road in the San Gabriel Mountains. They drove through the gate, and locked it behind them. This was the beginning of a lifelong project of learning to love and live with those who are radically different than us.

Before We Saw Blue:

memoire meets trail guide meets fantasy novella

There's a giant on Cadair Idris, and there's an American pastor who feels compelled to climb the infamous Welsh peak to challenge a giant. More than anything this is a battle for sanity. It is a trail guide to a real mountain, and a story filled with giants, and dragons, and faeries and hellhounds; and lessons on how we relate to past traumas.

Chasin' the Bard:

a pastor tries to keep up with Shakespeare

The great bard wrote 154 sonnets. This is the first of three parts of a project to does the same. These are sonnets on spirituality, love, betrayal with various influences from Welsh culture by the poet/songwriter/wanna-be philosopher who grew up in Southern California and migrated to Salem, MA. Each sonnet carries a description and details on its creation to help the less poetically minded among us.

You can find these other titles by the author on amazon.com

Phil Wyman is a Christian pastor with a rich history of relationship building with people from other religions and worldviews. Originally pastoring close to home in Carlsbad, CA, he moved to Salem, MA in 1999 to start a church called The Gathering. Here he began befriending the Witches and Neo-Pagans of Salem to break down the barriers of mistrust between the Christians and the Witches, which had developed over many years. His work with Neo-Pagans and atheists, and his forays into places like Burning Man has been highlighted on the Front page of the Wall Street Journal, in the Christian Science Monitor, Christianity Today, and numerous local papers and radio programs around the world.

Phil is a pastor, writer, editor, musician, songwriter, poet, wannabe philosopher, creator of interactive "blank canvas social art", and a general instigator looking for people to join him in a revolution.

If you are interested in contacting Phil for speaking engagements, gigs, becoming a team member in transformative festivals, or you simply want to connect to say hi and debate a bit; you can find his contact information at the websites BurningReligion.com, PhilWyman.org and SalemGathering.com

Phil is also a participant in a team of people helping Evangelical Churches relate to their neighbors from other religions in loving and redemptive ways. You can find out more about this project at MultiFaithMatters.org